Let's Go Do Some Mushrooms

- -

Short stories about experimenting with psychedelic mushrooms under different mindsets, settings, and dosages.

To submit your story please visit <u>DoMushrooms.com</u>

All artwork in this book was created and designed by the author.

PSYCHONAUT

A person who explores their own psyche through altered states of consciousness to explore the human condition.

Often with the use of psychedelic substances.

Disclaimer

This book is not intended to give advice, nor is it intended to persuade any person to partake in illegal activities.

Text in this book is not intended to encourage the use of illegal drugs.

The stories in this book are based on real events.

Names, dates, locations, and times *may* have been changed.

Preface

I don't know when it began, but one day I woke up with an immense fear of death. Not the event of death itself or the likelihood of pain, but with the uncertainty of what comes after. A heavy weight of anxiety slowly followed as I fell into a loathing despair. Amidst this fear, I truly believed that I was soon going to die. Rather than acknowledging its existence, I forced my newfound feelings into the farthest corner in my mind where they slowly began to grow. Before I knew it, the seedling grew, and it took over every aspect of my life. I became thoughtless, selfish, and passively harmful to everyone and everything around me. My fear then morphed into a paranoia.

When will I die?

I found myself hating who I had become. Depression, a word which carries little weight to its grips, took over my soul. And so, I did what most people do, and I ignored my own cries for help. After months of *dealing* with this burden, I decided that I needed to change. I missed the warmth of happiness and the excitement of being truly alive.

I missed feeling.

I missed love.

I simply, missed.

-

This journey began when I finally grew tired of hating who I had become. My search into psilocybin led me to both promise and skepticism. I, along with the majority of my generation, was raised on some variation of the same story which formed our current negative perceptions of certain drugs. For most, *bad trip* is immediately what comes to mind when thinking of psychedelic mushrooms.

What seems to fall by the wayside are stories with real impact—the types of experiences which make us contemplate the inevitability of life:

Mortality Afterlife Fear Love God

The stories that aren't discussed are the ones that I have found to be the most profound. The stories that make people feel like they've died and then safely awaken from their trip. The stories which allow people to see the afterlife through the clouds above. The experiences where you stand face to face with god.

Throughout my search, I discovered a large variety of stories and soon became addicted to their divinity. Unfortunately, I found it difficult to decipher which stories were real and authentic. I could not find the answers I was looking for.

I wanted real life. I wanted digestible and relatable experiences. I wanted to read them, and I wanted to talk about them—anything that would take me deeper and fulfill my curiosity. I wanted to have real conversations about ones consciousness before, during, and after a psychedelic mushroom experience. Ultimately, I wanted to see if these mushrooms could *help*.

I was jealous of those brave enough to alter their consciousness. In order to fulfill my curiosity, I had to experience it for myself. I had to see if I could feel transcendence. I had to see if I could experience death. I had to know if I could meet god.

This book encompasses personal stories from my point of view while under the influence of psychedelic mushrooms. I did my best to describe authentic, objective experiences that are in no way intended to sway your opinion.

Regardless of how in-depth these stories are, there is no way to fully grasp *this* reality without trying them yourself.

-    -

I believe American culture is stuck between two positions on psilocybin: 1) We either isolate it as something used solely for spiritual and medical treatment, or 2) we categorize it as a Schedule 1 drug which is reserved only for the black sheep of society.

It is my belief that the spiritual and medical factions are afraid of delegitimizing themselves by admitting the enjoyment of recreational use. Contrastingly, the free spirits of our society generally alienate themselves in a way that promotes ridicule. Why must it be so taboo for something to be enjoyable recreationally *and* provide spiritual and medical benefits? It's unfortunate that society has prematurely cast judgment on psychedelic mushrooms without truly understanding the topic.

Psychedelic mushrooms have undeniably influenced my life in a positive way. I have been lucky enough to experience the profound in ways that have altered my perspective until the day that I die. It is easy as a reader to digest these short stories, but it is impossible to truly imagine the journeys they've provided.

But why stop at the profound? Were my experiences spiritual and beneficial to my psyche?

Yes—but goddamn I had fun along the way.

Introduction

Do not be discouraged when reading words describing varying degrees of stress. Crisis, panic, crying, distorted reality, death, and any other thought-provoking descriptions have different meanings when someone is under the influence of psychedelic mushrooms. Throughout this book, some of the descriptions of emotions will seem intimidating, but in reality, they are moments of pure joy or intensity. As an example, crying on psilocybin is likely related to an incredibly beautiful experience. A feeling of crisis is likely caused by an event of immense intensity, often during the onset of effects.

-

Judgement is inevitable. Judging is easiest when we are in disagreement, or when we are in fear of jeopardizing our own values. We are most resistant to things we don't understand. In order to be receptive to new ideas, we must have a willingness open ourselves up to discomfort and accepting the reality of embracing the unknown.

It is my intent to provoke your thoughts and comforts as a way to make you, the reader, adjust your perspective. Throughout this book, if you find yourself disbelieving the various perceived realities, ask yourself *why* you are in disbelief.

Are you in disbelief because it goes against your current perceptions or values?

Are you in disbelief because you deny change?

Are you resistant because you think you have an opinion on drugs?

Are you scared of judgement?

Are you afraid to open yourself up to new ideas?

Have you actually contemplated what reality is?

Undoubtedly, you will form an opinion and maintain some sort of judgment. Whatever opinion or judgments you form from these short stories,

I hope they're actually *yours*.

Doses

The average reader likely has no gauge of reference when reading dosages for psychedelic mushrooms. No matter what your experience with psychedelics is, I suggest reading the below descriptions in order to have a better understanding of what weight correlates to the potential intensity of experience. Reference the glossary at the end of the book for questions regarding terminology.

The potency of psilocybin in mushrooms varies from strain, cultivation methods, and combination of both.

Dry weight and wet weight vary significantly in calculating dosages. It is generally accepted that psychedelic mushrooms (psilocybe cubensis) tend to be approximately 90% water weight.

I developed the weights below from my own experiences.

Dried Psilocybe Cubensis (in grams)

0.1 to 0.75 - Microdose.

You will feel capable to perform daily tasks.

You will likely feel a boost in creativity.

You will feel an enhanced appreciation for *things*.

You will likely feel agile, but odd, athletic ability.

You will know exactly what you are and are not capable of doing.

Regardless of the microdose, never underestimate the mushroom.

.75 to 1.5 - Introduction to Shroom world.

If you find yourself wanting to try psilocybin mushrooms but don't know how much to take…This is where you should start.

Things will seem different.

You feel it, but do you? You will ask yourself this throughout your ~ 4-hour experience. This will get you comfortable with what it feels like on mushroom mountain.

You will feel your jaw but only a little.

Things that are beautiful will feel *more* beautiful.

You will likely feel comfortable and lazy.

You will have full but lackadaisical control of your body.

You will not want to talk to strangers.

You will laugh a lot.

You will see a lot.

You will feel a lot.

1.6 to 2.0 - This is where you should not start.

Things around you **will** be different.

You will feel different.

You may see patterns in everything, you may not. You will, however, see *something*.

Day to day will be enhanced and you will be 'wow'd'.

Your reality will not be the same reality as it was before you took mushrooms, but remember, this is what you wanted.

You ate them, deal with it.

You are on a trip and it will be beautiful.

2.1 to 3.5 - You've been on a trip but now you're going on a journey.

Your reality will be **very** distorted.

Fractals, geometric patterns, kaleidoscope, breathing, feeling colors - it's all here.

You will have control of your body, but you are clearly affected.

You will feel a lot.

You will find it difficult to speak.

Time, space, and reality will be very intense.

You will have a true psychedelic experience.

You will feel love.

You will feel intensity.

You will feel more than you thought you could feel.

I hope you have the courage.

3.6 to 4.1 - Major distortions in reality. Major distortions in self - possible ego death.

I wrote possible, but it's likely. You need to have a guide. You should have a guide for all of the above mentioned but for this one, you will **need** a guide.

Speech will be impeded, greatly.

You will have control of your body, but will you *really*?

You will question things around you because your reality is vastly different than anything you've ever known.

If you choose to close your eyes and lay back, don't panic, you are loved, and say goodbye to yourself.

Try and let go; you will be okay.

4.2 to 5.0 - Complete dissolving of self.

The patterns? Here.

Beautiful colors? Here.

But you won't really pay attention to them because you'll be too busy trying to deal with...everything.

Ego death.

Goodbye earth, you'll be back later.

Goodbye self, you'll be back later.

Have a qualified spiritual guide.

You will learn things about the universe that you cannot un-know.

5.1(+) - Likely paralysis. You ain't doin' much, bub.

You're gone, probably for a while.

No danger to your body, but make sure you leave it in a safe place because you will leave this place.

Welcome to everything.

This book is dedicated to:

Sara

Gabrielle

Josh

Katie

Caleb

Hunter

Ani

Eric

Tobey

Jon

Emily

My father D.

My mother F.

Thank you.

<u>Table of Contents</u>

The Eye in the Sky
1.0 gram

The Spiral
4.2 grams

The Eyes and Faces
2.3 grams

The Mural
1.3 grams

The Pink Ocean
1.5 grams

The Space Station
2.0 grams + 2.0 grams

The Cuddle Bug
0.78 grams

The Freshie Boy
1 fresh mushroom

The Mushroom Eating Contest
1.2 gram + 1.5 gram + ? + ?

The Door, The Palace, & The Gods
2.5 grams

The View
1.5 grams

The Toe
0.5 grams

The Observer
3.0 grams

The Eye in the Sky

- Mindset: This is my first real mushroom experience. I wasn't nervous in the traditional sense, but I was nervously excited. This was Sara's first time consuming as well, so I knew I had to be extra prepared. Whether you're ready to admit it or not, there is always the fear of a *bad trip* before your first trip. Luckily, I was able to push the nervousness aside (or at least I thought I did), and I felt mentally prepared for whatever.

- Setting: There's a large patch of grass near the strand in San Diego, California. It's surrounded by beach-goers, vacationers, and cars driving through. It has a little bit of nature mixed-in with the modern world, so we could wander to the sand or roll around in the grass with the luxury of bathrooms near-by.

- Dosage: 1.0 gram each.

- Date/Time: Spring. 12:00pm.

- Method of Ingestion: Lemon TEK. Water.

- Strain: Mazatepec.

Event -

It's amazing that anyone can hop on social media and order drugs online from a complete stranger. In this case, *Mazatepec,* Psilocybe Cubensis. After paying $80.00 to a complete stranger, I felt as if I had thrown my money away. Without a doubt, this method of scamming happens quite often.

Within a week, I received an envelope from an ambiguous sender with what looked like a small amount of dried bluish stems and caps. Sara and I began to do online research on how to get the most out of them.

What we found was lemon *TEK.* Lemon TEK is the process by which smashed up mushrooms are placed in individual teacups and then soaked in fresh lemon juice for about twenty minutes. Sara and I thought we had a bulletproof plan. We packed a bag with snacks, fruit, water, juice, and a big blanket for a day at the beach. The plan was to simply take the shot of mushroom brew and walk to the beach, which was about a 45-minute journey. We thought that by the time we arrived at the beach, the mushrooms would kick in and we could enjoy the experience near the water.

What we found out after our journey was the enzymes in fresh lemon juice begin to break down the psychedelic compound in mushrooms, psilocybin, into psilocin. Psilocin is what causes you to *trip*. By using the lemon TEK method, we sped up the process to feel the effects of the mushrooms in less than half the time.

Sara and I looked at each other, cheered our glasses, and drank our cups dry. Immediately after ingestion, we grabbed our bags, and we started towards the grass patch near the beach where we could lay comfortably and enjoy the day.

As soon as our feet hit the sidewalk, we put the GPS on which showed a 1.7-mile walk. No more than 5 minutes from our doorstep, and much too far from our destination, Sara claimed to feel *something*. I too felt *something*; however, I knew immediately that I had a responsibility to keep calm. I knew that if I didn't, we would both be panicking after realizing we had a mile and a half remaining.

So, when she asked,

"Is it weird that I feel it already?"

I lied and said I didn't feel anything to (hopefully) buy us some time.

As we walked down the sidewalk, I noticed for the first time how busy the road was. Cars seemed noticeably louder than usual, and there was a feeling of busyness around me. Then, out of nowhere, our first signs of effects.

A car pulled off the main road and drove into a business behind us. As it pulled in, the tires made a slight skidding noise.

Sara and I immediately jumped out of fear and grabbed each other. We turned around and saw the car in a parking spot.

Nothing is out of place.

We looked at each other confused,

"Why did that scare us?"

I said.

Once we realized we jumped for no reason, we laughed. That's when we both knew we were in for a real journey.

I felt a climbing intensity in my stomach start working its way through my body. A slight anxiety weighed on my chest as we continued to walk. I learned later this is called the *come-up*. My vision, along with the world around me, began to change.

The hill to my right was no longer the same hill I had known for years. It's the same hill that I pass to get to the beach every day. But this time it was beyond beautiful in a way that I had never *felt* before. The grass, dirt, rocks, and trees on the hill began to flex up and down as if it was breathing. The hill swayed in every direction at once with no identifiable start point. A subtle undulation pulsed between the foliage and rocks. It became immensely beautiful.

To our left, palm trees in the distance resembled the shape of fireworks; the trees became massive. They were incredibly larger than I ever noticed before. They were the same trees, but somehow different. Their rigid trunks led to an explosion of marvelous bright green palm fronds on top. They, again, became impossibly huge.

Have they always been like this?

Sara and I looked at each other confused at the beauty of the landscape around us.

Well, I guess I'm on mushrooms now.

Even though we had drinks packed inside of our bags, Sara decided that she was craving coconut water. At the top of the hill, we mustered up the courage to walk inside a convenience store.

"In and out...

as fast as we can."

As we walked inside the store, the immediate energy around us changed. The interior of an un-natural building felt incredibly odd. It was as if I could feel how h e a v y the building was around me. The fluorescent lights blinded everything in a deafening pale. I felt our energy bounce off the lifeless concrete walls and come back to us. It was an uncomfortable and foreign feeling; we couldn't help but laugh while wandering around the store. I felt strangely weighed down by the interior walls. I looked at Sara, and I saw her slouching and then realized that I too, was slouching more than ever. The heaviness of the building took a toll on our physical bodies.

We bursted through the door into the fresh air, and everything felt so incredibly light outside. A wash of relief poured over me—we made it outside of the concrete prison.

Thank god!

I realized that my eyesight was far more intense than normal. Every movement from any object in my view became noticeable, but it was far too grand to digest everything at once. I entered sensory overload; thankfully, I remembered to breathe.

We arrived at our biggest challenge yet: a major intersection. Cars were flying by us at what felt like incredible speeds. The intersection exuded an immense intensity that became almost too hard to handle. Sara started making jokes about everything around us; it was clear to me that humor was a way for her to not panic at how much longer we had to walk.

As we crossed the intersection, I felt as if everyone around us knew we were *on mushrooms*. I looked at the strangers in their cars and a slight paranoia set in and it seemed impossible that they didn't know.

Are we walking weird?

Stumbling?

Laughing too hard?

No.

It was pure paranoia, an undeniable irrational fear that any common person could ever think or know that we were *on mushrooms*.

We finally made it across the intersection to our final stretch of road...And there it was. Something caught Sara's eye and made her stop dead in her tracks.

A palm tree.

The palm tree was overlooked by almost everyone who walked by it. Sara stood on the sidewalk—almost frozen—and her jaw dropped with a giant smile. I didn't really know what the big deal was until she pointed out the leaves and told me to focus.

I stared closely, and then I saw it the way she did. The palm fronds were blowing in the wind in a way I had never seen before. Each tendril swayed in every direction with an unfathomable amount of fly-always. There was no start or finish to the movement; there was no beginning or end. We tried our hardest to make sense of the incoherent beauty, but each palm leaf string was dancing impossibly fast, yet impossibly slow. It was swaying truly as if it was moving always, never, and forever.

"Do you see it?"

She asked.

I did.

I had seen palm trees a million times before, but this time was different. Was there wind? I don't know. We stared at that palm tree for minutes until we realized that we probably looked strange, so we continued walking.

We were no more than 50 steps away from the sand and water but still a little way from our final destination.

I could no longer feel my jaw but had no problem speaking.

I could no longer feel my legs but had no problem walking.

I was floating, without a doubt, and Sara felt it too. As we continued on our path, we talked about how detached we felt from our bodies.

Floating down the sidewalk there were large beach front homes on our left and in-between them the ocean was visible. The ocean view was massive, but only short lived because of the amount of ocean homes. At last, the houses ended, and we had a full unimpeded view of the vast ocean, and on it, a giant military ship. The ship shocked me and jolted my senses with instant intensity.

The ship is bad?

The ship is scary?

The ship was *something.* That something was not, in sober terms, good. My senses began to increase as I looked at all the metal.

Too much metal.

The ship stripped everything away from a view that could have been incredibly beautiful. I immediately felt the ship's energy as something born for destruction. Purely un-natural, in every sense. We refrained from acknowledging its existence from then on.

Finally, we made it. The grass patch. It borders the boardwalk, a cliff, the ocean sand, and a road. I don't think it would have mattered what our destination was, all that mattered was we made it *somewhere.* We were safe but more importantly, we felt safe. We laid the blanket down and collapsed on it. We exhaled with a sigh of incredible relief and realized that we could now fully enjoy the day. The trek was finally over.

We laughed. We talked about how hilarious the walk was. We talked about how distant the memory of the convenience store was, and we laughed some more.

Before I could get truly comfortable, I had to use the bathroom. I stood up to use the public beach restrooms about 50 feet away which was the arch nemesis of nature. The bathrooms were in a concrete cinderblock building with steel pipes, fluorescent lights, and people everywhere.

I got this.

I thought, as I prepared myself to go into the stall. I closed the door behind me to pee and realized that I was surrounded by gray cinder blocks.

Structure.

Fuck.

It felt odd to be in the concrete stall, so I took a deep breath. As I did, the walls breathed as well. They inhaled with me, stretching outward in every direction. They inhaled so much that it could have pushed the stranger in the stall next to me. I held my breath, in pure shock with my eyes wide open and looked around to make sure I was really seeing what happened. I finally exhaled and so did the walls.

Oh my god.

It really happened. There is no way it didn't happen.

I saw it.

I felt it.

I did it about three more times because my god it was incredible. I played with the fluctuating walls with excitement and disbelief.

I beelined back to Sara who was having a blast looking at the grass. I told her all about my endeavors of making the walls bounce. She laughed, but she was too distracted to give me the time of day. Sara had something more interesting to talk about. That's when she introduced me to grass world.

"The grass is hilarious."

Sara said.

I agreed, in slight confusion.

I stared at the greenery to really see what she meant.

There was a whole world in it, sand, bugs, a city of busyness and vibrant entangled blades of green. Grass world was full of life. It was living, breathing, and moving. It shared none of the characteristics of *building world* which had no semblance of life. Concrete and cold. We laughed at grass world while looking at everything in it. There was a certain giddiness that came with staring at tiny ants weaving through their day.

And for whatever reason, we were done with grass world and we decided to lay back to watch the sky.

Then we saw it.

But it became clearer and clearer as we continued to watch it unfold.

Sky world.

If there ever was a phrase which carried littler weight to the profundity which it meant, sky world was it. Sky world seemed impossible, in every context.

Like clockwork, a kaleidoscope tunnel presented itself at the same time and detail to the both of us. A massive pulsating ring of colors manifested in the sky above in the same detail and area to us both. Chuckling at the beauty, we described what we were seeing to each other which strangely, matched.

How is it that we both see the same thing?

The more we stared at the kaleidoscope tunnel, the more the sky opened up. It unveiled itself as we continued to look. After all my years on earth, I was finally able to see the sky for what it is. An impossibly large dome made up of symbols resembling 6's, 9's, and cursive jagged R's. Hieroglyphics encompassed the horizon in every direction.

It showed itself slowly.

First, you could only see the details near cloud cover.

After 10 minutes of looking, it all became realer than anything I had ever seen.

From horizon to horizon, the sky was made up of some sort of seemingly ancient grid-like pattern. It seemed clear to Sara and me that the sky was made of the symbols both in *shroom world* and the sober one.

For me and my eyes only, the sky revealed a room in what resembled a Celtic-style wooden library without any books. It was very clear to me that I was looking into the *next place*. I didn't see much into it because *it* didn't want me to, but it was both near and impossibly far away. I inspected it for what felt like hours, and I marveled at its intrinsic beauty. I *felt* that I could only see very little into this room because I was not yet brave enough to ingest the number of mushrooms needed to be granted access. It showed me just enough to pique my interest into what else lies behind the curtain.

I felt tiny. Impossibly small in relation to this next place of unfathomable magnitude of distorted size.

I had just reached the pinnacle of my journey. I was in bliss of all the new things I uncovered that day. I was somewhat still coping with the knowledge of *now I know these things exist and I cannot un-know them*. Things were beginning to dwindle down, so I thought.

That's when I saw it.

The Eye in the Sky.

Clearer than looking at my own hand.

Clearer than anything I had ever seen in my entire life.

More detail than anything and everything, I was staring at it, and it was staring at me. A massive eye in the sky. It felt as if it was my own eye looking back at me from above, but I knew that it couldn't be. I felt cognitively rational enough to know that it wasn't my eye, but I also knew that it was real. I could see it just as clear as the plants and humans around me.

I was struck by its complexity and simplicity and I believed in it. I knew what I was seeing was real because it was real.

Isn't that what real is?

In between the clouds and perfectly straight above me, the eye gazed down at the earth. It existed, purely, without movement or hesitation—completely still. The eye was hazel with seemingly normal eye lashes and had no prominent features, which was the most intimidating component. It wasn't magnificent nor was it beautiful. It wasn't colorful or marvelously impossible. It was simple.

It was solely an eye doing exactly what it was created to do. Look.

I told Sara about the eye, but she couldn't see it and I realized the eye wasn't for her; it was somehow for me. After a long period of inspecting the eye, it began to fade away.

4 hours into the experience, but also a lifetime later, the trip was over. We gathered our stuff and called a ride home. Driving back, we laughed at how far we had walked. We eventually got home and had no struggles coping with the things we saw because, well, we saw them.

After all we had went through, we were starving.

So, we did what most humans do: order pizza.

The Spiral

- Mindset: What originally piqued my interested into psilocybin mushrooms was the possibility of overcoming my fear of death. I can't pinpoint when this fear manifested, but it sent me into a self-destructive depression for months. It wasn't the event of death itself that scared me, but rather the uncertainty of what comes after. This fear had been in the back of my mind before this trip, but I refused to acknowledge it. Nonetheless, it acknowledged me.

- Setting: Living room couch.

- Dosage: 4.2 grams.

- Date/Time: Spring. Typically, I record the time. This event was so intense that I have no true recollection of when I ingested.

- Method of Ingestion: Lemon TEK. Ginger tea.

- Strain: Golden Teachers.

Event -

There is no doubt that psychedelic mushrooms taste bad. They're horrible. Acidic, earthy, fleshy, and gritty. A part of me thinks they taste so terrible because there needs to be a balance of good and bad. For them to provide such powerful experiences they must taste horrible.

At that point in my life, I felt pretty comfortable with mushrooms. I took what I believed to be respectable dosages in a variety of situations. I ventured into different methods of ingestions and dosages under very different settings. Though my experiences have aways been vastly different from one another, I never had an experience that made me truly hesitant to take them. That's when I decided to take 4.2 grams.

There are some generally accepted considerations that a person should have when ingesting mushrooms— mindset, setting, and dosage. Mindset is arguably the most important. When preparing your mindset for a trip, it is recommended that you have an intention going into an experience. Perhaps focusing on a new perspective or maybe you're trying to overcome some sort of fear. Unfortunately, for me, everything I did leading up to the ingestion was far too complacent. I didn't have much of an intention and even preparing for my tea was lackadaisical.

I didn't grind up the mushrooms very much; they were more like large chunks of cracked mushrooms than chopped bits. Looking back, I was indeed much too cavalier about taking such a heavy dose.

I should have *respected* the mushroom.

Standing in my kitchen, I used the butt end of a butter knife and lazily chopped up the dried stems and caps. I squeezed in some lemon juice and let the mushrooms soak. After a few minutes, I poured some boiling water on top and mixed in ginger tea. I remember noticing that there were more mushrooms floating than I was used to.

The nervous feeling produced by a combination of digesting enzymes and pre-trip anxiousness is a chemical cocktail of emotions commonly referred to as the "come-up". The come-up from 4.2 grams was much more intense than anything I had experienced thus far. It was incredibly hard to handle. Nausea—pure nausea—set in within minutes of finishing my tea. During the come-up, I started teetering back in forth from understanding reality and not. Pink fractal kaleidoscope patterns replaced any semblance of what I knew to be the walls of my house. As strange as it may sound, I felt as if the mushrooms wanted me to lay down. It felt like I didn't have a choice; I had to lie down, and so I did. I laid on the couch, and I looked at the ceiling without any concept of how much time had passed.

Everything in my vision became intrinsically morphed with shards of unidentifiable geometric shapes.

Patterns became evident in the walls and ceiling, but with a bolder texture than previous mushrooms trips. I could *feel* the geometric patterns and textures with my eyes. The visuals of shapes were familiar, but what wasn't familiar was blinking. Every time I blinked, I got a flash of intense colorful beauty. Naturally, I started to blink slightly longer and longer out of pure curiosity. Then, out of no where, my blinks went from 3 seconds shut, to 5 seconds shut, to completely closed.

I witnessed a tunnel stretch into the infinity. An infinite amount of pure color was pulled *down* into a spiral of color abyss. I suddenly felt myself falling, slowly, into the infinity. I quickly opened my eyes to make it stop.

Once I opened them, I was no longer falling. I was relieved that I was able to stop my soul from departing. Curiously, I closed them again and the same thing occurred. The longer I closed them, the longer and deeper I felt myself getting pulled toward the center of the infinite. It felt as if my soul was getting pulled through the earth without any resistance. I prepared myself for the journey and said out loud to Sara,

"Hey..

I'm leaving but..

I'll be back."

I do not know if Sara replied.

Let's see where this goes, I guess.

I felt my soul get pulled from my body, downward, in, and through. I didn't just feel it, I also saw it get pulled. As I fell through the couch, I reminded myself to not forget about my body. On earth, I moved my hand onto my chest to feel my skin and heartbeat. After feeling the comfort of having a heartbeat, I then fell through the floor, through the ground, through the energy of the earth.

I saw myself, not my body, but my real self fall down and in. My soul was falling slowly down an endless swirl of mixing colors. I *felt* the colors just as strong as I saw them.

Deeper

and

deeper.

I was going *IN.*

I write *IN* because as I fell through, the letters I and N ran across the swirling abyss of colors with truly no beginning and no end in existence. An infinite IN.

Ginormous I's and N's perfectly straight resembling a text box on a computer screen.

I felt as if my body no longer existed on earth. I could not feel my chest nor my heartbeat—my hand no longer existed.

My breathing ceased.

My body became irrelevant.

I thought to myself.

I over did it.

I overdosed.

While my soul spiraled down the abyss of colors, I told myself that I had overdosed on mushrooms. I truly believed it. I believed that I was now completely dead. Almost immediately I became resistant to the idea of not existing, but I knew in my heart that my life was over. It was an irrefutable fact that my body on earth was gone and I had to be okay with it. I was, however, overcome with sadness that I wasn't able to say good-bye to my loved ones. I thought about my family and grew incredibly uncomfortable *dealing* with the pain. My sadness left because I knew that I could not go back. I tried to push the thoughts of loved ones away to not have to deal with the pain of losing them. All of these emotions came and left in a cyclic wave of heavy emotions as I continued to fall down the spiral. The longer I fell, the slower I fell *in*.

My life on earth is over.

I reached the bottom, or the center, or wherever was the end of my falling. I was struggling with the idea of letting go. Resisting the idea of no longer being alive. I fought it; however, my attempts were futile. I wanted to push back, but I didn't know how to fight it.

I was stuck.

Dead but conscious.

Aware but nowhere.

Gone forever.

I knew I had to let go but I was scared.

Terrified, I decided to leave this world behind. I prepped my consciousness for departure.

Finally, I let go.

As soon as I accepted my death, I detached from existence and exploded into pure energy. *I* was no more. *I* was now a part of everything and anything.

I, was.

My death was followed by pure silence and nothingness.

There, is where *I* was for an inexplicable amount of time.

-

My eyes opened back on earth and pandemonium shortly followed.

I'm alive now?

How am I alive?

Am I in my house?

Where am I?

I was just dead, so how was I alive? I leaned up from my couch, confused. The walls were pink, but I was home.

Am I a person again?

I had forgotten my name and my identity.

Do I have a name?

I did not know my name.

Do I live here?

I did not know my house.

I looked at Sara and I did not recognize her.

Just as I sat up, she, like me, just woke up from the dead. She too, ingested 4.2 grams and was just as confused as I was which confirmed my confusion. We were lost.

No identity.

No self.

Just alive.

"I'm confused."

She said. I repeated the same.

We couldn't say much more than 'I'm confused' for quite a while. We wandered around the living room, grabbing our heads in confusion.

She began to cry out of fear. I began to cry too. Pandemonium. Psychosis. Disarray. Delirium. The onset of a nightmare panic and psychosis set in amongst the confusion.

I knew I had to help her, but I didn't know who she was. I was in a great amount of emotional pain and so was she.

"Do we live together?"

She asked me.

"I don't know, but I think so?"

After knowing each other for 10 years, we had forgotten each other—truly forgotten.

"Is this our home? Do we live together?

Do I have a job?"

I asked.

"I think my name is Amanda."

Sara replied.

I felt the need to introduce myself to her. I didn't say my name, but we shook hands.

The confusion lasted what felt like a loop of eternity. Constantly battling through remembering and forgetting our previous lives. Sara continued to cry, and we embraced as awkward strangers. I cried, then she cried, then I cried, and we wept back and forth.

Time went on.

"Oh my god, we did mushrooms!

We did too much…is this a bad trip?

I think we're having a bad trip!"

She solved the puzzle during a point of clarity. But it wasn't that easy. She quickly slid back into psychosis and was taken over by emotional pain. Soon after, I slid back into delusion and insanity before coming back to a glimpse of sobriety. Over and over, we battled between delirium and reality.

The mind of an insane person is undesirable in every sense.

I looked toward the kitchen, walls, and couch with no true understanding of what they were. I was no longer filled with any bit of understanding of what, was. My environment was filled with unknowns in every possible sense. Colors and patterns added to the confusion of unknowingness.

Please make it stop.

We took turns being there for each other, trying to snap each other out of pure insanity. I can't tell you how many times we cried that day. It was painful, grueling. We addressed how painful the experience was, even while going through it.

We walked outside and sat down on the patio floor. Sara looked at me crying, and she knew I was going through a tough time. At that moment I didn't know how describe the pain of losing my identity other than crying. I was crying but I didn't realize how much pain I was in until Sara acknowledged my pain.

I looked at her with tears in my eyes and said,

"I'm sorry."

I was sorry.

Any and every bad, terrible, and disgusting thing I had ever done flashed through my mind. Sorrow poured out of me like a wave of emotion. I was disgusted with myself for all the wrongs I had done in my life. All my regrets played in my head, over and over, showing me the pain I inflicted onto others.

Any time I lied in my life, I felt it. Any time I stole in my life, I felt it. Any time I wronged someone, I felt it.

I relived every lie I had ever told. I relived every time I stole. I felt the pain of everyone I had wronged. Pounds of guilt fell into my stomach with an unbearable weight of emotion. I witnessed my wrong doings as an objective bystander and felt the pains of my mistakes.

I was terrified of the lostness.

I was scared of the un-reality.

I felt true sadness.

I felt true pain.

Over the next few hours, we managed to crawl back into reality. It was a gradual climb, but we made it out. It was devastating both emotionally and physically.

However, I don't regret it. I did lose something that day, and what I lost is only for me to know. I can tell you that I did see myself and hated what I saw.

I do wish I was better equipped to deal with the issues that had arrived. I do want to go back *in* but next time more prepared.

Six months later and I'm still not ready to go back that deep.

Scared? Yes. Terrified.

And you would be too.

The Eyes and Faces

- Mindset: Excited, thrilled, exploratory. I wanted to explore. I wanted to look at plants and have a greater appreciation for nature. Three friends and I planned this adventure weeks in advance. We mentally prepared ourselves for the dosage of mushrooms we were going to eat, knowing it was a hefty dose. I didn't have my phone with me; I didn't have responsibility, but I did have three close friends and nature.

- Setting: Sequoia National Park, Hume Lake, and a creek which led to waterfalls. The creek flowed through our home base toward the lake. You couldn't wish for a more perfect day.

- Dosage: 2.3 grams each.

- Date/Time: Summer. 11:00 a.m.

- Method of Ingestion: 2.3 grams ground up and put into 13 vegetarian capsules. Ginger beer as a chaser.

- Strain: Golden Teachers.

Event -

The four of us planned to have a mushroom experience in Sequoia National Park. However, the details were very loosely planned. We packed all of our things into two cars and set the GPS to Hume Lake. After the long car ride, we found a perfect spot to set up camp.

We had nothing to do that day but explore aimlessly through nature. We had chairs, fruit, food, drinks, and pool floaties to enjoy during the experience. Off the main Sequoia road, we found a trail that had a variety of beautiful tall trees and luscious green scenery. Parallel to the trail ran a creek which had a plethora of ideal staging areas. We spotted a perfect nook near one of the creek rock pools and plopped our things to get ready for our journey.

We each cracked a ginger beer.

"20 minutes till blast off!"

We put out blankets for a cozy laying area where the trees met the creek. Nobody was around and we had miles of forest and water to explore. Our safe spot. Our home for the day. We were only about 100 feet from our cars, which made it easy to grab some extra blankets or snacks if need be.

We all cheers'd at 11:00 a.m. and swallowed 13 pre-weighed mushroom capsules each.

"See you guys in a few hours!"

We all sat around our safe spot and talked as a way to burn time until the effects kicked in. After some casual conversation and small exploring of our area, I began to feel nervous. I couldn't tell if it was actual nervousness or the come-up from taking a large dosage (more than likely the latter).

The come-up hit us hard about 40 minutes after ingestion. It was so powerful that I can't really tell you exactly when it kicked in, but it did. We were in one of the most beautiful places on earth; so, even soberly, the views were impressive.

The still cold water reflected the sky above and the rocks below became visible. The result: a reptile skin pattern.

Is everyone seeing this water?

Whenever you're witnessing something incredible, especially on drugs, you try to get everyone around you to experience it. I tried my hardest to make the reptile skins as relevant as possible, but the group slowly drifted into their own experiences.

Sara told me that she was starting to feel nauseous. My instincts kicked in, and I had to do whatever I could to make her feel comfortable. I told her that I would run to the van quickly and grab her a ginger beer for her upset stomach. It's hard for me to imagine a simpler task, walk 100 feet to the van, grab a ginger beer, lock the van, walk back.

"Are you sure you're okay to go over there by yourself?" Sara asked.

I told her that it was no problem at all. As I gathered my things for a quick trip to the van, I felt the intensity rise inside me. I reminded myself to focus as hard as I could— at least until I could retrieve the ginger beer for Sara.

I walked up the trail and made it to the road. To my right, the vastness of Sequoia Forest. To my left, the same. Straight ahead was Hume Lake, which was impossibly beautiful to describe. After realizing the magnitude of the forest around me, the onset of *panic* began to kick in. The beautiful intensity of colors poured over my vision, and it became hard for me to comprehend the world.

Things are different.

Back by home base, I watched the creek become more beautiful; it was a gradual transition. The creek was safe; I knew the creek. This was different.

I was not ready for this magnitude of beautiful. I also didn't account for the 5 minutes that passed looking for my keys and sandals to walk to the van which meant I was 5 minutes *deeper*.

At the road, I could see the van across the street. I looked to my right and saw the forest hill stretch impossibly long for what seemed like an eternal distance. There was a point at which the tops of these giant trees met the sky—I wasn't prepared for it, but I kept looking. It was intensely beautiful. Too beautiful. Too Much.

Beautiful to the point of burden.

I took a deep breath.

S l i g h t panic.

Ginger beer. Focus.

I stopped myself from the immense distraction of panic. I looked down to keep my focus, and I walked across the road. By divine happenstance, two strangers approached me right after I stopped myself from experiencing a beauty induced panic.

"Excuse me, is there a trail down there?"

Fuck.

Did I say fuck?

Did I say anything?

Oh, no.

They were speaking to me.

Or, wait, are they?

Who are they?

I took a moment to think as they were standing in front of me. I stood there wondering if they actually asked me something. After an eternity of a long pause, I realized they were waiting for a response.

I then realized how long it had been since I said anything, which made me laugh at the awkwardness. Then I laughed harder.

Then I laughed, *really* hard.

I was staring at these strangers point blank and laughing in their faces which made me laugh, again! I tried to say something but there is no way that I could. I accepted that as fact and just walked away from them. I'm certain that they were confused which had to have made an interesting story.

I made it to my van. I unlocked it, found the ginger beer, and grabbed one for myself.

I had done it.

But wait, it's not over.

The world was getting more and more *shroomy* by the second. I locked the van and prepared for my journey back.

I turned around to start walking and swore to myself that I wouldn't speak to anyone until I got back to the group.

Did that really happen?

Did I really just crack-up in the faces of complete strangers when they asked me for advice? I absolutely did.

I made it back and sat down with my group. I did it, I really did it. I couldn't wait to tell them what I had accomplished. For me, it felt like I just went through the craziest situation of my life. I felt like I had so much to tell them. But how? My jaw barely worked, so I just started blurting out my story.

"..you guys wouldn't believe what I just went through."

I tried my hardest to tell them my story, but jaw felt like it was made of honey. The mushrooms hit me with a wave of the new reality. That's when I realized how anti-climactic my story was. In a nutshell, I walked to the van, laughed at strangers, and walked back.

What kind of shit story is this?

I realized the blandness of my story mid-way through which made me start laughing. My punchline was received by three blank stares; they didn't get it. Their blank stares reminded me, of *me,* when the strangers tried talking to me by the road.

Blank stares; six eyes staring at me in pure stillness. The reaction made me panic laugh.

Oh no, it's happening again.

Their stares made me laugh unbelievably hard—I could not stop.

I was having a laughing attack which turned into a laughing panic.

My laughing panic turned into a laughing crisis.

My laughing crisis turned into a laughing cry.

Am I weeping?

Sara, Eric, and Ani watched me with blank stares as I laughed myself into a crisis cry. I realized that they too, were *tripping* hard. I then realized the effect of me laughing into a crying crisis could easily put *them* into a crisis. So, I did what I did before near the road. I laughed in their faces and went on a walk.

I needed to deal with my crisis alone.

I began wandering up stream. There were rocks, waterfalls, trees, dead trees, new trees, old trees, and everything in between. I kept wandering, slowly climbing from rock to rock. I looked in the frigid cold water and saw a stick, so I reached in and grabbed it.

The water doesn't feel cold anymore.

The stick was now a part of me, and I used it as a third arm. I could navigate through the rocks, in and out of the water, with no shoes, no discomfort, and no consequence. How? I don't know. My feet were still my feet, but they had no pain. I could still feel them but at the same time, I couldn't.

The water was beautiful.

The land was beautiful.

The trees were beautiful.

I squatted on a rock using my third arm for balance and thought to myself.

This is what I wanted, and I got it.

My intent came through. I wanted to be in nature and really experience it for what it was. I looked in the distance to take it all in.

I breathed, it breathed.

The water met the rocks. The rocks met the trees.

I looked up.

The trees met the, sky?

Why is the sky different?

Why is the sky, not the sky?

More precisely, why was the exact point where the treetops meet the sky seem like a *replica*?

I kept looking. I squinted and stared to digest my vision. I realized that there was a point of stoppage where far away trees and far away sky met. The stoppage point hadn't *composed* itself yet, as if I caught the sky taking a break, from being the sky. It was full of distant pixels. Blurry pixels which hadn't become clear because no-one was near them or no-one was looking. My world was now a low-quality computer screen. And so, the world around me became digital.

I had to be okay with it.

I wandered relatively far from home base. I remembered my original intent of wandering was to deal with my crisis. It was dealt with but more importantly, I was okay with the new digital world around me. My crisis subsided to the point of self awareness. The come-up was over and it was now time to enjoy the journey.

I approached the group and looked at everyone objectively. Ani was staring at the water with a smile on her face. Eric was looking up and staring at a tree branch. Sara was laying on the blanket, smiling. I approached Eric and asked how he was feeling, and he replied with the most appropriate response,

"I looked at this branch and I was going to break off this

twig, but I couldn't.''

Realizing how funny it sounded, he smiled and continued

"It seems less of a big deal now... but a couple seconds ago it was a way bigger deal."

I knew how he felt.

Twigs, man.

I walked over to Ani and asked her the same. She replied with a giant smile, barely able to squeeze out the words

"..there are two fishes..

And..

They're great."

Fishes, man.

It seemed now everyone was at a high level of *shoomery*. There was an even playing field of immense distorted reality to which only those experiencing it could ever understand. We each shared a commonality of meaningful perspective which no one else was granted access. After feeling confident that our group was safe, I walked over to Sara and asked her to wander with me upstream.

We took the forest route. We were immersed in a

sea of trees both dead and alive. We witnessed the greenest green there ever was. Our feet were bare; neither of us so much as got a splinter. The ground felt exceptionally padded, bouncy almost. I crawled and climbed over and under in ways I wouldn't usually. I became more flexible and felt my body personify more animalistic traits. I strangely felt like an animal.

Monkey.

I don't know when it started or what my first sight of them was, but *they* seemed to come out of everything. *They* became visible in every place I chose to look. *They* made up anything and everything.

Eyes and faces, all around me.

It sounds terrifying in retrospect, but it wasn't. They were all around me, passively existing.

I said it out-loud,

"All I see are eyes and faces."

I felt the eyes on me, but they were objective. They were non-judging. They did not have the capability to judge or to not judge, there were simply there. The smallest stick and the largest rock were made of eyes and faces. The river rocks were skulls, the trees were a collective of an impossible number of faces. I inspected crevasses or things around me with odd shapes just to see if they were there. They were. They knew I was there but showed me no sign of life.

It was a message. From whom? Or what? Impossible to know for certain. But I knew then and there that I was being watched at all times by everything in the universe. Every poor decision that I had done or will do was being witnessed by them. I thought of my past deeds: sincere, sinister, and ones of love. I was slightly ashamed that my negative actions were witnessed by *them*. It's one thing to believe that god witnesses all with the consolation that you don't have to face him daily. It's another to witness the universe witnessing *you*.

We explored upstream for what felt like days of wonder. We were explorers having the time of our lives. Under trees, through rocks and sand, we wandered up and down the forest. Sara noticed the most perfect dandelion on the edge of the creek. It felt right to pick it, so she did. Our intent was to blow and spread the seed as far as we could, as was it's purpose. We inhaled and blew with all the power our lungs could produce.

Nothing. No change. Not one single white parachute.

Sara was astonished at the dandelion's ability to remain strong. It was if it was not yet ready to release its seed. It now fell under Sara's protection; there was no way she was losing that dandelion. We both felt like we had to share it with home base. We felt the need to share our experiences with our group.

"Let's go back to Eric and Ani."

We walked downstream, through rocks and over trees. It felt like we walked for hours, enjoying every minute of it. No sunburn, no dehydration, no muscle aches, no splinters, and no cuts on our feet. It was a miracle.

We were close to camp and I could see Ani and Eric doing exactly what Sara and I were doing, wandering aimlessly. We all locked eyes and our jaws dropped because we found each other! It was like a reunion! It was as if we hadn't seen each other in weeks. Our groups were too excited to say anything, so Sara picked up the dandelion to show Eric and Ani the massive ball of white parachutes.

As she lifted it, *p o o f*, like magic. Every single white parachute miraculously dissipated into the calm wind. To everyone else on earth, this is no big deal. To Sara, it was a miracle.

There was what felt like weeks of experiences we wanted to share with each other. Each of us individually, lived through days of wandering. We tried to share as much as we could, but at the same time, there was still so much to see. We decided to keep wandering, but this time we wandered as a group. Sara and I led Eric and Ani up stream, through the rocks and sand, through the forest route of dead trees and alive ones. We showed them the padded forest floor. I told them about the universe of faces and eyes around us. We shared our experiences as we wandered up stream where the dandelion once lived.

We came to a point where we had to walk across rushing water. Usually, when we were crossing moving water there were rocks to hold onto for balance or at least some floor sediment where we could dig our feet in. At this particular spot there was only slippery rock and no place to grip. In a straight line I was the guinea-pig and crossed. I turned around at the group and saw the horror in their faces. To them, it was impossible to cross. The mushrooms flexed their perceptions of the rushing water and the distance to land on the other side. In their eyes, it must have been miles.

Hilariously, the gushing water was a mere 4 inches deep. To them it seemed far too difficult of a task.

Eric was up next,

> "Alright man give me your hand and I'll help you across."

I told Eric.

"I don't know man; I don't think I can make it across. It's too crazy."

He said.

I started to laugh because I understood that this crossing in his mind probably seemed incredibly difficult but, in all reality, the water passage was about 4 feet long. Laughable to the sober mind.

"You got this man, just give me your hand!"

He hesitated but agreed.

He wobbled and moved slowly—ridiculously slow. So slow that any onlooker would have assumed Eric had a balancing issue. After what felt like an eternity of wobbling and shuffling, he made it across.

Ani didn't even attempt the crossing. She continued straight up the path and found an old dirty rope, which kept her occupied while I tried to convince Sara to cross. Sara stared at the crossing and decided then and there that she wouldn't even try. She backtracked and took the longer path around and made it to the other side.

I looked back at Ani holding the rope and her posture changed as she wrapped it around her body. She personified an explorer as if she had taken on the identity of a paleontologist, looking for artifacts.

The effects began to wear off as we reached the top of the creek. Naturally, we consolidated as a group and began conversing about our final experiences, attempting to grip onto what was left of our *trip*. On the walk back, we talked and laughed at our adventures. We were astonished at how impeccable all of our feet were.

How is no one injured?

As we walked back to home base, we laughed at areas which were difficult to pass. We couldn't believe how safely we walked up and down the stream throughout the day. Back at our home base, we checked the time; it was 3:00 p.m.

How is this possible?

We were now perfectly sober. Fully energized, fully self aware, and complete control of our cognitive abilities and muscles. We looked at each other and asked,

"Well, now what?"

We packed our stuff and drove an hour to the biggest tree on earth.

The Mural

- Mindset: I wanted to feel creative—artsy, if you will. It's not that I don't feel like a creative person; I was more curious to see what would happen if I were to take some mushrooms and paint. The idea was to take a dose, blast music on speakers, and spray paint what ever came to mind on my garage wall. Since I was taking a pretty light dose, I wasn't nervous about this experience.

- Setting: My garage is 50 feet long and approximately 9 feet high. It's a relatively large space with very bright white walls. The house was a new construction, so the garage looked like an empty canvas. I played a variety of musical genres to influence creativity.

- Dosage: 1.3 grams.

- Date/Time: Spring. 7:00pm.

- Method of Ingestion: Ginger Tea poured on crushed mushrooms.

- Strain: Golden Teachers.

Event -

This was one of those ideas that someone thinks about but would never actually carry out. The type of idea that comes to you when you're hanging out with some friends and someone says,

"What if you took some mushrooms and drew something?"

Luckily for me, I was curious enough to try. I ran the idea by Sara (she liked it but didn't feel like taking part in the adventure). Nevertheless, she was happy to provide emotional support as a babysitter.

I mashed up the mushrooms in a teacup and poured boiling hot ginger tea on top. After letting them stew for a few minutes I finished the tea and decided to prep my area in the garage. I laid out a large 12 by 12 sheet of plastic to stop the mist of residual spray paint from sprinkling on the concrete floor. I set up my speaker and made an impromptu playlist with the intent of having a multitude of genres for cause and effect. With no plan set, I stared straight at the tall white walls and felt pure sobriety while holding a can of spray paint.

Should I just start now, or should I wait?

I waited… largely due to not having any ideas. I had no idea what I was going to paint. Where do you even start on

a blank canvas with no ideas?

The answer is: you don't.

Water.

Surely, I'd get thirsty. I convinced myself I wasn't procrastinating so I walked upstairs to get some water as part of my "preparation". As the cold water hit my stomach, I felt the mushrooms. The familiar rollercoaster of nervousness became prominent and I was ready to hop on. I quickly poured another glass from my fridge spout and walked downstairs to the garage to get back into the zone. As I walked through the door to my garage, I felt the cold energy radiating from the concrete floor. I stood in front of the blank canvas and stared at the oddity of white walls.

Pink. I love pink and I'm not afraid to say it. Fluorescent pink, hot pink, bright pink, pink pink. I love pink. Naturally, I grabbed pink to start.

But now what?

I stared at the pale blank walls and still had no inspiration. I shook the can, which felt strangely tiny in my hand.

Then, I noticed my hand did not feel like *my* hand. The oddity of *your* hand not feeling like a part of you is a subtle feeling of detached bodily transcendence. It ceased

semblance of possessiveness and solely existed. *My* hand independently existed as one of something other than identity. My hand was now, a hand. Or, and likely most accurate, it became and only ever was, hand.

I shook the can again, and that's when I truly felt the mushrooms.

Just start.

My visual distortions weren't ones of color or beauty, but of size and depth perception. The wall in front of me grew in height and width.

Am I little now?

I looked left, down the long side of the garage and witnessed the walls extend farther and farther away from me.

The light reflected against the white walls which contrasted the darker concrete floors and gave a feeling of cold lifelessness.

This place needs color.

I lifted the can and began spraying aimlessly. Pink, everywhere. Blue, everywhere. Yellow, everywhere. Up, down, center. I continued to spray large paint globs of dripping vibrant sheens. I spray painted over and over until it started taking shape into swirls. Swirl after swirl the wall took shape into a tunnel. A tunnel with no stoppage, full of bright blinding color.

I looked left and again witnessed the cold lifeless passage which encouraged me to add more vibrance. I swirled the pink in a tiny circle and slowly encompassed the entire wall. Then again with the blue. Then with yellow, orange, red, green, every color overlapping the last. The mural developed into a large swirling tunnel of vibrant colors, forever long and full of life.

I felt the mural was similar to my life in some aspect. I have always felt sorrow in the inability to stop time, even for a second. We are all spiraling through space, time, and color with no possibility of stopping our deaths. During our journeys through life, we grab hold of whatever we can for structure, whether it's a home or a memory just to *get a grip*.

I drew a house in the center. A home. A tiny home representing some structure in the forever spiraling abyss, giving me something I could hold onto. Then, I added a man next to it spiraling down the abyss unable to *get a grip* or remain intact. It looked how I needed it to.

It reminded me of us: every human in the world just trying to get a grip or hold on to anything. I grabbed my **black** paint and inscribed the words in giant large letters:

Just a tiny world hanging on for dear life.

The Pink Ocean

- Mindset: This experience wasn't planned. I had no intention of taking mushrooms that day, but I agreed to be a babysitter for Gabrielle. After seeing what a wonderful time she was having, I decided to join her. Coincidentally, my brother was in town which took off any pressure to be a babysitter. Overall, I was mentally comfortable (largely due to having a close friend and my brother with me as a safety net).

- Setting: The majority of this trip took place at my apartment near the beach. At the height of my experience, we all went to a cliff which overlooks a vast panoramic view of Carlsbad beaches.

- Dosage: 1.5 grams, each.

- Date/Time: Spring. 12:00 p.m.

- Method of Ingestion: Lemon TEK.

- Strain: Golden Teachers.

Event -

My brother Josh came into town for a visit. At this point in our lives, he had no idea I had been experimenting with mushrooms. For years, he had been trying to get me to take psychedelics with no success. We had previous conversations about LSD, but the opportunity to take it never presented itself. I was never really that interested in LSD. Something about synthetic compounds just doesn't interest me as much as something born of nature. Josh had always been more mature than me when it came to altered consciousness, so I was excited to share my experiences.

The morning after he arrived, I told him about my recent endeavors with psilocybin mushrooms. He was thrilled to hear it and we exchanged stories about past experiences. I asked him if he'd want to <u>do some mushrooms</u> with Gabrielle and me, which he declined. He did, however, offer to babysit. I originally decided not to partake, but that changed shortly after Gabrielle took a dose. After seeing her having such a phenomenal time, I was taken over by my jealousy.

I squeezed some fresh lemon juice and let the mushrooms marinate in a teacup for a short while. The come-up was casual. Nothing too intense, but not nothing at all. I've found that you will always experience some sort of intense buzz or a subtle nervousness that brews in your stomach.

Josh and I started to play video games on the couch while Gabrielle was entirely in her own world. I looked at her sitting in the corner near the patio door and she had a plant pot in her hand. She was both crying and laughing as she cupped her hands. After some investigating, she was holding a dead mosquito. She lifted the pot and had a small funeral for the mosquito and then buried the insect out of respect. She looked at us and said,

"There is no way you could understand."

I'm more of an explorer when I'm on mushrooms. I don't know if it's my body coping with the new reality that I'm witnessing, or if I become curious.

Nonetheless, I wander. Gabrielle and I walked out the front door of my apartment and sat on the stoop. Our view wasn't much in the traditional sense. We could see the sky, but we were surrounded by the apartment complex. Concrete exterior tan walls in every direction, all with textured concrete finish. The textures were primarily large smears of exterior mud. On a normal day, the building was nothing notable, just an apartment complex.

We started to notice subtle changes in the texture. The muddy abstract smears began to take shape. Lovely cupids and small cherubs shooting arrows manifested through the smears. Not realistic, not cartoony, not animated, but subtle prominence in the actual texture. Lips formed from other smears, swaying and moving in different directions. They moved slowly with a sort of dignified beauty. It was lovely. We looked up at the sky and noticed the subtle beauty of ancient patterns. *Sky world* was there but we had already experienced it during a different adventure. Before we became captivated within the intricacy of the sky, we quickly moved our sights to the cherub show on the breathing building walls. We sat with our backs against the wall, and our knees leaned on each other. It was truly intimate, and we felt the love surrounding us.

Josh came outside to check on us. He was wrapped in a blanket and snacking on grapes.

"Whatcha' guys doing?"

He said as he smacked his lips.

We described the beautiful cherubs and different small breathing images in the walls. He replied with the most monotoned and unimpressed tone,

"Oh wow.....cool."

He kept chewing.

"What else you see?"

We described the immense sky world, the textured patterns everywhere, and the ability to see into the universe above us which was naked to him.

Again, with almost zero care he kept chewing grapes,

"cool, cool...

Sounds cool."

We died laughing. Such an appropriate reaction from someone unimpressed or impeded by the revelations we were experiencing on mushrooms. Everything about his tone and mannerism were unbelievably unsurprising to someone who couldn't comprehend what we were witnessing. He was just too human. Hilariously human.

I couldn't resist an adventure,

"Let's go exploring!"

I was Gabrielle's arch-nemesis; she wanted nothing to do with walking around. She wanted to lay down and enjoy what was in front of us. Luckily, I prevailed. We gathered our things and hopped into the truck with the beach as our destination. I was safe, but more importantly, I felt safe. I felt loved. I had my best friend Gabrielle sitting right behind me and I had my brother driving. There was no possibility of worrying in the world.

The car ride is blur to me. If I try hard enough, I can still remember laughing and snippets of vivid nature view. Somehow or another, we ended up in a dirt parking lot on top of a cliff which over looks the ocean in Carlsbad. Fortunately for me, I hadn't noticed the ocean view yet. We parked, got out of the truck, and walked towards the cliff.

Ironically, I find myself in that very parking lot at least 3 times a week. It's one of my favorite surf beaches in southern California. I know everything about this cliff. I knew the water, the tide, the walking paths…everything. But that day it was different. It was as if I had never experienced it before.

The ocean was the ocean, but it was larger. Impossibly larger, impossibly immense. The water became bright pink with shades of dark reds and light purples. I felt the beauty overwhelm my senses as a weight formed in my throat. It was beautiful to the point of shock at which I could almost not handle. The magnitude of the pink ocean overloaded my senses of being able to experience. My throat began to feel tight. The ocean water and backdrop sunset was as magnificent as I would imagine god intended it to be. I felt my emotions climbing through my sinus and *almost* poured out.

During this overwhelming emotional experience of witnessing the ocean, Gabrielle walked up behind me and hugged me. The love pushed me over an emotional edge. There was nothing I could do to hold back the tears.

Love.

I felt loved.

We stood there watching the pink ocean in silence. At that moment, I saw the ocean for the first time in my life. I had the gift of re-experiencing the water the way it was intended it to be experienced.

I cried with pure joy.

I felt true love.

I saw true love.

The Space Station

- Mindset: It was what I would describe as a "normal" Saturday. I knew earlier in the week that I would be taking mushrooms that day, so I made sure I had no plans. For some reason, I felt very interested in space leading up to ingestion. Perhaps, I recently watched Interstellar or some Alien documentary—who knows. What I do know is space was on my mind.

- Setting: Throughout the duration of this trip, I spent the majority of my time in three locations: Passenger in my golf cart, a garden by the ocean with vibrant plants, and on my couch.

- Dosage: 2.0 grams + 1 hour + 2.0 additional grams.

- Date/Time: Spring. 11:00am.

- Method of Ingestion: Lemon TEK. Cup of ginger tea.

- Strain: Golden Teachers.

Event -

    Before this trip I had been researching the effects

of psilocybin in great depth. *Intent* was what stuck with me. By focusing on a specific subject or focusing on what type of experience you would like to have, the mushrooms will manifest it (in theory). Having an intent is generally accepted in realm of consuming psychoactive substances.

Space. For some reason, the days leading up to this trip I kept thinking about space. In what context? I still don't know. But Space was undoubtedly on my mind. Up to this point, I'd only ever had wonderful mushroom experiences, so I thought, why not up the dosage?

I chopped up my mushrooms and let them soak in about a centimeter of fresh lemon juice. After 10 minutes, I poured boiling hot ginger tea on top in order to kill any unwanted bacteria. I grabbed my cup, and Sara and I walked to the golf cart in my garage. The most I planned to do that day was to drink the mushrooms, drive around town, and look at plants. Sara agreed to be my babysitter.

Near my house in San Diego, California, there's a hill which S the surrounding neighborhood and ocean. It's one of my favorite views in all of San Diego County. So naturally when Sara asked,

"Where do you want to drink your tea?"

The hill came to mind.

Sara and I hopped in the golf cart and drove to the hilltop.

We parked, I swallowed my tea, and we sat for a minute enjoying the view. There was a tiny portable speaker on the golf cart, so I put on the Beatles for background music. We sat for a few minutes listening to music and enjoyed the scenery. It was a beautiful day, not a cloud in the sky and just cool enough for a light jacket. Sara asked,

"Well, now what do you want to do?"

I shrugged my shoulders.

"I guess let's go for a ride".

We took a right through the neighborhood which is a 5-minute drive to the main downtown strip. I was looking around in every direction eager to see my first signs of life.

The come-up was a mild intensity. I felt it strong in my stomach and felt a small amount of nervousness as the mushrooms digested. Wondering when your drugs will kick in will forever be one of the greatest questions.

What will I notice first?

We were now a block away from downtown and I began to feel the anxiousness really kick in. My eyes widened and I gripped onto the armrests, bracing myself for mushroom impact.

Sara noticed my posture and asked,

"Wait, what do you see?!"

Mushrooms typically don't make you see things that aren't *there*. There are no cartoon dragons or gremlins. You don't see flying cars or monsters. You do, however, see an enhanced distorted reality. You feel and see *things* that are impossibly real which makes you question everything. Nothing looked different but things felt different. Weird is the best way you can describe your arrival to that place. Things still are what they are, but they're just more of themselves than usual.

I looked at the surrounding landscape. Streetlights and buildings seemed different but with no physical change, at least from that perspective. We kept driving and turned on a very busy road. The whole downtown area has a speed limit of 35 MPH, so I felt safe on the cart but having no doors was a little nerve wracking.

We made a left on the Pacific Coast Highway. Palm trees bordered both sides of the road, perfectly spaced apart and impossibly large. I began to feel the intensity and magnitude of the environment around me.

Why are these trees massive?

I looked straight ahead and witnessed the road continue on straight for what seemed to be infinitely long. There were buildings, businesses, cars, trees, and roads on a straight line that went on endlessly with no horizon in sight. Absolute endlessness.

I turned around to look behind us and got the same result. The road behind continued on forever.

I couldn't believe how far it went.

I couldn't believe how far I could see.

I couldn't believe the vastness of distance.

The road had an impossible amount of space.

Knowing that things around me were getting intense I blurted out,

> "Let's go to that one garden patch by the beach and look at plants."

I couldn't have been more excited to see nature in this new reality. We zoomed through turns and I felt like I was on some sort of strange human safari. The world around me was changing rapidly and the intensity in my stomach extended throughout my body.

We arrived at the garden and it was more beautiful and foreign than I remembered. Bright blinding blue flowers. The most beautiful blue I had ever seen radiating in the grass in front of us.

Echium Fastuosum Candicans.

How do these exist?

My jaw dropped. Figuratively, because I could not feel my

jaw at this point.

Are these alien flowers?

We pulled over, and I jumped out to inspect them. A vibrant blueish hue radiated as an aura surrounding each flower pedal. If a bomb went off 30 feet away, I would have protected this shrub.

How are people ignoring these flowers?

I was now seeing life in what I think is comparable to *sepia*. A colored lens fell in front of my eyes and all I could feel was this new world. Everything around me in this new reality was one note of *color*, aside from *colors*. Red was red, blue was blue, but every color had a filter of sepia attached to its surface.

Is this the real world?

I was now fully *on mushrooms,* but I wanted to see more of the new reality. I wanted to go deeper.

"Let's go home really quick. I want to do some more."

With excitement on her face, she agreed.

Not more than 5 minutes later, we zoomed into the garage. I wobbled upstairs and ingested 2 more grams as fast as I could. Life as we know it is filtered. Our minds funnel out a significant amount of noise. That noise is, for lack of a better term, the unfiltered universe.

The higher the dose someone ingests, the less of yourself exists within that noise. Letting go of your perceived "control" of the universe is a scary feeling but, I was ready for more. I was ready for space.

"Let's go back."

I said, laughing.

She obliged and we went back into the garage and sat on the golf cart.

We jetted right past the hill where we started.

This cart feels way faster now.

Flying on the cart we made a right and a left and we were back on the main road once again.

Intensity ensued. The palm trees, bigger than before. The buildings were no longer buildings, they were docks. They changed shape and meaning.

Space docks.

The cart also changed shape and meaning. It was now a buggy.

Space buggy.

We were flying down the super space highway at incredible speeds. I felt the road as a space highway because in a way, it is a space highway.

Cars everywhere were now space mobiles on their own journeys on the planet. The roads off the highway led to other neighborhood planet space docks. We were weaving through a sepia space highway going a million miles an hour.

My perception changed with no warning and everything became impossibly warped.

The road was no longer down. The road was up. We weren't driving down a road, we were driving up a road.

The street in front of me became a 90-degree angle, up. Looking forward felt as if we were climbing up the side of the road, the same way you see ants walk up a wall. I looked back and behind us was *down*. If I jumped out of the space buggy while driving *up*, I was certain I would fall down through space. Ear to ear I was smiling larger than ever.

This is awesome.

Left, right, left, right, zooming through the neighborhood roads, I was describing what I was seeing to my space buggy driver (or trying to).

Straight was up, back was down, and I was in no relation to anything.

How am I driving up... if space is up?

Then it dawned on me, we *are* in space. I was suddenly able to comprehend the earth in with a different perspective.

We are all walking, driving, and living, hanging on to the side of the planet; we're just little. My perception of what I was feeling was justified. Society's established directions are from our perspective as humans and are meaningless in the eyes of the universe. Up to someone in California is sideways to someone in Antartica. Any direction is omnidirectional with a large enough distance between space. This made sense to me now, no matter how silly.

I walked around more plants and continued thinking.

> *Green? Green does not justify green enough.*

> *Flowers? Impossible to comprehend.*

> *Direction? It depends, from what perspective.*

We hopped in the space buggy and drove back into the garage, which was no garage. It was a docking area for the space buggy. I walked upstairs to the living room; on a normal day, the garage is inside the house.

Not today.

Today, my inside living room was outside. I plopped down on the couch near the windows to think about all I had just witnessed in space. I contemplated all the revelations I learned about time, distance, and direction.

Enough thinking.

I needed to enjoy the view while I could.

I sat up, walked to the patio and gazed at the distance contently. I could see the hillside in the distance. Hills were now mountains and the mountains went on forever. Cars were flying by in their space pods on whatever journeys they were doing that day. Staring at the view I soaked it in. I engulfed myself in the world of sepia color and space buggies.

I inhaled and exhaled trying to truly grasp the beauty.

I stared and enjoyed the planet.

It was just another Saturday, on Earth.

The Cuddle Bug

- Mindset: This was my very first time ever consuming mushrooms. I did a lot of research on what to expect, but I was still nervous. No amount of reading can prepare you to distort your reality for the first time. This was it. All my research, planning, and preparation came down to that night.

- Setting: Sara's family home in West Palm Beach, Florida. I grew up with Sara's family, so I was comfortable with the setting. Earlier in the evening I told Sara's whole family what I was planning on doing, and they were supportive, which alleviated any emotional pressure. My close friend Hunter agreed to take the same dose with me so that I was comfortable throughout my experience.

- Dosage: 0.78 grams each.

- Date/Time: The eve of a very popular winter holiday. 10:00 pm.

- Method of Ingestion: Raw dried mushrooms and a glass of water.

- Strain: Unknown.

Event -

This was my very first mushroom experience. Honestly, I just wanted to get it over with. The more I talked to friends (and friends of friends), the more I kept getting fed horror stories. Though these stories were discouraging, I wasn't interested in rumors. I tried my luck on the internet, but anytime I searched "what to expect," terrifying psychedelic experiences filled my web browser. Instead of relying on others, I chose to shut the computer and see for myself.

I asked my friend Hunter to join me for my first journey and he happily agreed. Hunter is very experienced with psychedelic drugs and has a rock personality—a calm but firm presence. The type of personality that wouldn't really tolerate your crisis. Or rather, the type which makes a crisis seem silly.

Earlier in the day, I received a text message from my friend Jon offering me 1.5 grams of mushrooms. He told me to swing by his house around 9:00 p.m. to pick them up, which I did. Even though it was quite late in the evening, I knew I wouldn't be able to sleep that night without eating them. All the research and pre-trip anxiety culminated, and I knew that I couldn't wait another day.

I picked up the *shrooms* and nervously put them in the cup holder of my car. I asked Jon and his wife, Emily, if I could pay for the mushrooms. They declined the money and told me,

"The first one is always free."

As I drove back to Sara's house, I kept looking at the tiny plastic bag. I couldn't believe how scared I was of what looked like a couple of bluish-tan crumbled bits. My anxiousness increased as I got closer to Sara's, and I finally told myself to stop being a baby.

Hunter was already inside and was waiting for me with a scale ready to divide our dosages.

"How should we take them?"

I asked, nervously.

"Just eat 'em."

He said. Nothing fancy—very Hunter-like.

As he spoke, he popped the batch into his mouth like they were crackers. He had zero hesitation. His cavalierness put me at ease and as I ate mine, a sense of relief came over me.

There's no going back now.

I was no longer worried about *when* I was going to do

them. All the horror stories didn't matter now, because there was no going back. The deed was done; good or bad, the experience was coming.

It was a crisp winter evening, so we set up a fire in the backyard and made some hot ginger tea. We sat in front of the fire and bundled up with cozy blankets to keep warm. It was now the middle of the night—quiet, calm, and comfortable.

An hour passed and we were enjoying the fire in silence.

First signs of distortions? Maybe?

There were trees, shrubs, and bushes 30 feet away from us which led to a heavily wooded area. Pine trees were tall. Seemingly taller than usual.

They were swaying in the night sky; well, their silhouettes were. I was sitting back in my chair and watching their tops dancing back and forth with the wind. I kept staring and realized they were all swaying in different directions. That's when I realized there wasn't any wind.

Am I overthinking this?

I followed a tree down its trunk to see how accurate my vision was and saw a bush nearby. I became determined to see if the trees were indeed swaying. I stared at the bush to see if it was also swaying with the non-existent wind. I squinted and stared. Hunter kept talking to me, but I phased out his voice to focus on the bush.

I stopped him mid-sentence,

"Sorry to interrupt you man, but I have to see if this bush is moving because I literally cannot tell."

He laughed—this was a situation he'd clearly fallen victim to in the past: a bush bamboozling.

I stood up and walked over to the bush and stopped two feet away to really focus on it. The darkness engulfed everything beyond it and my surroundings dissipated. I stood there, face to face (face to shrub) in perfect stillness. There was nothing else in the known universe; all that existed was me and this bush. I stared quietly and perfectly still. Not a single muscle on my body moved as I focused with all of my attention on the dark green silhouette. Still, no matter how hard I tried, I could not tell if it was moving. Strangely, I felt it moving without seeing it move. Checkmate, it defeated me.

I walked back and sat down next to Hunter and he asked,

"Well, was it moving?"

"Shit man, I still have no idea. For some reason I literally cannot tell. This bush is driving me nuts."

We burst out in laughter.

Behind us, we could see Sara's family in the kitchen cleaning up. Hunter and I went inside for *whatever reason*. As I walked in, Sara asked how I was feeling. I said good and giggled while getting cozied on the couch.

She was surprised. She was surprised because I was acting differently than what she was expecting. She was expecting me to go mad and freak out. She was expecting the worst most horrific *bad trip*. She was expecting me to lose my mind for 6 hours and fall into the grips of psychosis.

The opposite occurred. All I wanted to do was giggle, solve the mystery of the moving/not moving bush, and get cozy on the couch.

This wasn't what I learned about shrooms.

I laid on the couch and put on some headphones. I turned on music and told myself to accept whatever the mushrooms wanted me to see. The kitchen eventually cleared. Hunter went into his room, and Sara went into the shower. I was alone and gazing at the beautiful Christmas tree lights. Swaying gently, the tree moved in *every* direction. The silver Christmas tree ribbon caught my eye as it began to slowly morph.

What's happening?

Years ago, one of my closest friends, J., passed away in an accident. It was my first experience with death. It was, and still is, the most painful experience of my life. The event and how it affects me is painful but watching the emotional torture of my loved ones is far greater. The agony suffered by each person I love caused me to bury my feelings. I never dealt with this pain, thus cultivating my fear of death. There were days where I tried purposefully not to think about *him* because the burden was (and is) too difficult to bear. One of my greatest fears is knowing that he is watching me make mistakes in my life, which one day I will have to answer for.

-

The silver Christmas tree ribbon formed the letter "J". Was it a sign from above? A sign from beyond? Or was it a sign from my inner self telling me that I had unfinished emotional business? Regardless, I learned my feeble attempts to push my pain away were no longer possible. The "J" was the undeniable symbol of strength I needed to put the past behind me.

Finally, I relaxed and fell into my music with my eyes closed. I giggled every so often because things felt *weird.*

Eventually, Sara got out of the shower, and I followed her into her room.

I had no filter, because I didn't care to.

"I want to cuddle. Can we just hug in your bed?"

She laughed.

She agreed and we crawled into bed.

I was now a leach. I leached onto her in every way. Every part of my body was pressed against her.

"Uhmm, haha, are you okay?.."

She laughed

"..I literally feel your entire body wrapped around me. I can even feel your toes curl around my leg like they're hugging me."

Sara fell asleep, but I stayed awake for a while. I felt her warmth on my skin, and I felt happy. I laid quietly, and I felt a sense of gratitude for the wonderful evening I had. But mostly, I felt a sense of curiosity for the message I received.

Eventually, I fell asleep.

The next morning, I knew it was just the beginning.

The Freshie Boy

- Mindset: I was lucky enough to get my hands on a single freshly picked Golden Teacher mushroom. More than anything, I was curious. I was curious to see how one fresh mushroom would affect me. Moreover, I wanted to eat a fresh one without knowing the dosage (in order to have zero expectations).

- Setting: Passenger seat of a car and inside a restaurant.

- Dosage: One whole freshly picked mushroom.

- Date/Time: Spring. 10:00am.

- Method of Ingestion: I brewed ginger tea and dropped the entire mushroom in my cup. After 10 minutes, I ate the freshie and drank the tea. Side note: The fresh mushroom tasted much better than a dehydrated one.

- Strain: Golden Teacher.

Event -

    I had the opportunity to get my hands on a freshly picked golden teacher mushroom. This was my first time eating a fresh one straight out of the ground, so I was quite excited.

Sara told me she wanted to go to a restaurant that morning, so I asked her if she would mind if I ate the mushroom. Luckily for me, her sister was in town, so they were happy to babysit while I experimented. I brewed a ginger tea and plopped the entire mushroom in a mug to let it soak. After stewing for a few minutes, I drank the tea and ate the mushroom in two bites.

We gathered our things and walked out the door. The restaurant was about 40 minutes away, so I sat quietly in the front seat while Sara and her sister talked. We never discussed it, but it was understood that I would be in my own zone throughout the day. Sara would check on me every so often to make sure I was doing fine. Every time she checked on me, it was the same way—a light touch, smile, and a

"How ya feelin'?"

It was comforting.

As we were leaving the house, I could feel the come-up brewing in my stomach. It was a light intensity but still very noticeable. Toward the end of the drive, I was completely *on mushrooms*.

As I sat in my seat, I noticed that my legs felt odd. I could feel them, but I also couldn't. They felt like my legs, but they also didn't feel like my legs. More simply, they were just legs.

I was wearing shorts. While looking at leg hairs coming out of my thigh pores, it seemed like a silly system.

These hairs don't constitute, me. They are not a part of my personality or what makes me, me. They are just a part of this meat and bone vessel.

I looked closer and marveled at the beauty of how perfectly spaced out each pore was from another.

I wonder if it's more significant that they're perfectly spaced apart rather than random sporadic accumulation of pores?

I became more curious about *my* body. I started inspecting my arms.

My skin is peach colored, but why?

Almost translucent, but also not.

I observed my veins, pores, skin, flesh, muscles, tendons, bones. I curled and stretched my wrists.

This isn't me, this a body.

This body is a vehicle, not an entity. It was just something I use to get around.

The idea of having a soul is nothing new, and I had contemplated it a thousand times before. But this was the first time that I understood that idea. The idea that we are not our bodies. Even though whoever or whatever *we are* is not our bodies, that doesn't mean our bodies are less important.

I observed *my* hand and looked at *my* palm. My wrists. My arms.

How ridiculously flimsy.

Well, fragility is the point isn't it? If we were built indestructible, we would care much less how we treat ourselves.

Fragile. My body felt incredibly fragile. It is the only known *thing* to host our souls, and yet we treat them so casually. I looked at how frail my skin and bones were. I was more delicate than I had ever realized. That's when I felt that I had an absolute obligation to take care of my body.

How or why did I come to this revelation? This is something every functional person with a brain knows: take care of your body.

I'm not taking my body for granted.

We arrived at the restaurant. I took a deep breath and stepped out of the car. There were cars everywhere, people on sidewalks, packed restaurants, and bars on every corner. The area defined congestion. I was experiencing a mild sensory overload, but I was prepared for it.

All I need is a deep breath.

I followed Sara upstairs to the rooftop table. I sat, smiled, and looked around.

I was transported into the new place—the mushrooms world. I was now an outsider looking into the human universe. I was not a human, I just happened to be in a human body for the day. I felt like a ghost observer looking at all the humans around me engaging in what they call *life*. I stared at people enjoying their meals and company which gave me a warm sense of happiness. I found enjoyment watching humans enjoy their own experiences. Waiters, waitresses, patrons, pedestrians— I saw them all engaging in life harmoniously. What these humans forgot to know, and what I became aware of, was that nature does not stop. The earth is still there, nature still exists, and animals still hunt, regardless of how congested or civilized humans get. From the rooftop view, I could see nature in its purest form. Squirrels were climbing on telephone lines, waves were crashing on the beach, and insects were gathering their supplies. Their survival is dependent solely on food—a luxury humans think they're entitled to.

Rest assured, humans, that nature is still there and if it chooses to, it will show you that you are no different.

I ordered vegan eggs benedict with English muffins and jelly spread. I had a slight panic when it was my turn to order because well, the waitress was looking right at me. For a second, I thought I was caught not acting like a human. Luckily, I kept it together.

The food arrived shortly after, and I devoured it. The idea of eating food for which your body then converts into energy felt odd. I inspected my bites before engulfing them. The *oddness* of the food quickly left once I tasted it. Pure deliciousness.

The idea occurred to me that wasting bites of food was incredibly thoughtless. I imagined the journey that a potato goes through leading up to arriving at a plate. I imagined the act of planting a baby potato. I imagined the water it takes it took to grow. The weeks of earth, wind, and water. The miracle of survival—just to be sliced and put on a plate for a patron to carelessly throw away because they ordered too much. I was slightly disgusted at my own waste of food.

We paid, left, and were back in the car driving down the highway. I felt the breeze from the open car window, and I closed my eyes. While my eyes were closed, I saw how fast we were driving in complete darkness. Somehow in the darkness behind my eyelids, I felt the world passing by on the highway.

Shards of light started to fly by my head in the darkness. At first, I couldn't see what they were, but after some concentration, I saw red lips. Cartoon red lips blowing kisses blew past my head as if they were road signs. Bright colorful neon red lips zipping by without giving me a chance to observe them closely. Just as one flew by the side of my head another would show up and shoot past my other side. Mesmerizing. The notion of opening my eyes and ruining the beauty was immensely undesirable.

Throughout the day, I was fully functional and capable of performing easy weekend activities. I was, however, a little more *connected*. I learned from this experience that each mushroom trip is give and take. There is a direct correlation between how high your dosage is and how connected you are with *everything*. In turn, this disconnects you from your sober reality. You do not become incapable; rather, your perception of things that actually matter changes. The significance of self dwindles while the comprehension of pure existence increases.

Since that day, I do yoga daily. Undoubtedly, due to the already known revelation that my body is important.

Thank you, perspective.

The Mushroom Eating Contest

- Mindset: This was my friend Tobey's first *true* psychedelic experience. I felt slightly responsible for him, so I knew I had to be mentally sturdy before and during the experience. Knowing that he trusted me for setting and dosage, I provided him with comforting reassurance.

- Setting: The majority of the day was spent at my home near the beach in San Diego, California. Throughout the day, we visited the local downtown area and got driven around on a golf cart.

- Dosage: 1.0 gram + 1.5 gram + ? + ?

- Date/Time: Spring. 11:46 a.m.

- Method of Ingestion: Lemon TEK. Ginger Tea.

- Strain: Golden Teachers.

Event -

There are very few people I bring into the mushroom world. Not because I feared my safety or judgment, but because of my fear for their safety and judgment. Unfortunately, mushrooms are still taboo. Less taboo, absolutely, but still taboo. I don't talk much about psychedelics casually because frankly it's illegal. Also, you don't really know what someone's reaction will be. How does one bring it up to friend for the first time?

"Hey bro, *Let's Go Do Some Mushrooms?*"

Doubtful.

I was sitting at a bar one night in Downtown Carlsbad with my friend Tobey, and I grew the courage to tell him about a mushroom experience I had. Luckily for me, it fell on excited ears. He then told me an experience he had on a small dose of mushrooms right out of high school. Summed up, his experience was primarily in a dark room with night lights, music, and deep conversation, which he enjoyed.

I told Tobey that I knew where to find mushrooms and asked if he'd be interested in having an adventure. He was, indeed, very interested. Fast forward to spring.

Tobey is a go with the flow kind of guy and not much really gets under his skin. We didn't plan much, but we had the basics: mushrooms, a babysitter, a safe place, and sober transportation. Our plan was to eat the mushrooms, get driven on a golf cart, look at plants, and find some grass to lay on.

Naturally, he was pretty nervous leading up to ingestion, as this was his first *real* time since high school.

"No more than a gram bro, seriously, I don't want to go super hard."

He insisted.

I tried telling him, but he wouldn't listen.

I said,

"Bro, you're going to eat a gram and when it hits you, you're going to be like 'dang, this is awesome, but I wish I took more.'"

He wasn't convinced, so we agreed on one gram. At the end of the day, I was wrong. Anyone experimenting with mushrooms should **only take the dosage they are comfortable with.**

We Lemon TEK'd. After 20 minutes, we poured boiling hot tea and let it steep. We cheers'd and gulped it down. Talk about a being a baby—he kept gagging at the taste and was barely able to swallow them. Honestly, they're not that bad.

Sara, Tobey, and I went downstairs, hopped on the golf cart and took off. Things were normal for about 30 minutes as we explored around the neighborhood. I wanted him to see the blue flowers, Echium Fastuosum Candicans, so we went there. I may have miscalculated the timing because when we arrived, we were still stone sober. They were beautiful but still, just flowers in his eyes.

I guess they're not fully kicked in yet.

Nevertheless, those bright blue flowers will forever have a special place in my heart.

We kept driving.

I watched Tobey start looking around curiously.

"I feel like the wall is moving? Is it or is it not? I can't tell?"

Tobey said.

I checked my watch.

Right on time, 40 minutes in.

Such a relatable thing to hear.

"I've been there bro, the walls are definitely moving."

Things were nice. Calm, nothing crazy. We did however, start to feel lazy. Very, very, lazy. We drove to a patch of grass near the beach near downtown Carlsbad.

Standing up from the golf cart was incredibly difficult. We

s   l u   g   g   e   d

ourselves off the cart and

d   r   u   g

our feet onto the grass patch and finally plopped down.
Our necks hung on our shoulders out of sheer laziness as
we attempted to sit up from the grass.

"Bruh, what are these shroooms? I feel like I've been in
a jacuzzi my entire life and just got outtt."

Tobey said, almost slurring his words.

We laid on the grass, like drunken slugs. Sara put
down the blankets and we rolled onto them with minimal
effort. I then felt my depth perception changing, maybe
even warping.

Am I seeing... in fisheye lens?

My focus was prominent but warped and bent along my
peripherals. Our bodies became magnetized to the floor.
Both of us, strangely, had no desire or motivation to do
literally anything at all. Walking? Running? Jumping?
Yeah right.

Any movement or roll on the blanket was
emphasized with a massive amount of drooping and

sluggishness. Our laughter, however, was not impeded. Every sluggish movement was hilariously emphasized with an extra bodily droop.

We. Were. Useless.

"I literally cannot do anything. Geeze Lance, I didn't know we were going to be homeless for a day."

We laughed hysterically. I laughed so hard that I had a suddenly felt the need to pee. Luckily, or unluckily, there was a bakery on the corner.

Dare I?

"Alright guys, you're going to hate me but…I have to go pee. Anyone coming?"

Tobey slow-motion rolled and face me with an incredible stale face,

"Seriously bro. "

We slugged our way off of the grass patch, laughing the whole time. We were without a doubt walking through invisible wet cement. We opened the door to an adorable French bakery and as a shock to me, I felt comfortable inside. Things did feel odd, but I was okay with it. Tobey bought an orange juice and a pastry while I used the restroom. I cannot speak for Tobey's pastry eating experience, but he seemed to be emotionally invested in that slice. We left the bakery and just as I expected,

"I want more, should we take more?"

I knew it. I knew this would happen.

"Bro, I told you this would happen!"

But hey, what else did we have to do that day. Literally nothing. We agreed to up the dosage and see what happened.

Now, the hard part.

We slugged our way across the street to the golf cart. The drive back to the house seemed a little more intense for Tobey. He seemed a little tight while he gripped onto the armrests. He chose to sit on the passenger seat as a way to feel safe while I faced backwards on the cart.

We made it home and drooped our homeless selves upstairs.

"How much do you want to take?"

I asked.

"Maybe the same amount?"

He replied.

I explained that our tolerances were now elevated so we'd have to increase the dose. After some back and forth and minimal contemplation, we settled on 1.5 grams each. We didn't feel like doing the "whole lemon tea thing" so we chewed them up and swallowed them.

Boredom isn't a thing when you're on a mushroom trip. A room, a plant, a piece of paper, a stick, anything and everything has an incredible amount of wonder and amazement to it. We were sitting on my couch, no music, no TV, just us in a room. We were laughing and enjoying our surroundings while describing all of the things we were experiencing.

Tobey was now in full mushroom mode,

> "Dude, you HAVE to see the floor! Look at this is spot one the floor bro!"

All he wanted to do was watch the bending and elevating of the textured floors become three dimensional, as he described. I, however, was undergoing my own experience.

Colored geometric fractals and textured patterns manifested on the walls. The laminate floor began to undulate and breath with no repetitive cycle. Snake skinned walls surrounded the living room showing tiny figures, faces, cupids, angels, *breathing* in/on/throughout the wall. As I was enjoying this cyclic pattern of endless breathing Tobey interrupted,

"Dude, let's eat like two more mushrooms."

Fuck it.

I grabbed two, he grabbed two, and we scarfed them down. Sara heard us from upstairs and she yelled while laughing and in disbelief that we were eating more,

"Stop! Fucking! Eating! Mushrooms! You guys are crazy!"

Too late. We were cracking up, gulping down our water.

Who knows how much time passed.

But also, time? Time was longer relevant. We started talking about space, aliens, rainbows, and colors. We were sharing experiences about the geometric patterns manifesting on the walls surrounding us. And for the love of god, he still was trying to get me to stare at the floor.

I don't know why this happened because we were both clearly tripping. Tobey said,

"Dude, I want to see some SHIT. I want to eat some more."

I don't know if I thought it or I said it out loud,

"Seriously bro, you want more? You want to see some shit? Fine."

I grabbed a mystery amount, mashed them up, and walked over to him.

"You want to see some shit? Drink this."

He did.

Hmm. That was kind of a lot.

We decided to order sushi and pick it up on the golf cart to further the adventure. We placed the order for pick up and after 15 minutes, we hopped in the golf cart. For whatever reason, I brought a skateboard with me and buckled it in.

I do this drive frequently. Left up the hill, beautiful view, make a right, follow it down to the strip, left, right, boom! You're downtown. Tobey rode in the passenger seat next to Sara because the world around him was likely vastly different than it was earlier. My reality became incredibly distorted, I couldn't even imagine his.

Like a camera zooming out quickly, my soul was immediately sucked deeper as the golf cart peeled down the road. Deeper in mushroom world as the mystery dosages were finally digesting. A large unstoppable smile manifested on my face as a colored lens fell in front of my eyes. I looked around, gazing at the astonishing landscape of the city in disbelief. I looked to my left and to my right as we kept driving. Palm trees pulsed pass me as if I was in a tunnel. I looked at my prevalent peripherals and could feel the trees beating through my chest. The world around me was now one of a different plane.

We arrived at the sushi restaurant. Eating during a psychedelic experience isn't to satisfy hunger, it's to experience the oddity of food. We arrived early so the food wasn't ready. We took over a portion of the sidewalk as we waited. Tobey, still sitting in the passenger seat, wasn't moving. The intensity of the mystery dose was clearly affecting him. I found solace on my patch of sidewalk with my skateboard in hand.

A light green tinted shade overtook my reality. The beauty was deafened by the busyness of the downtown area. I looked right; the city life was moving in all directions. People, cars, trucks, and pure infrastructure raised my senses to an overbearing pressure of intensity. Every car engine, passive conversation, and white background noise cut through my senses in an overwhelming gradual inclining screech. Every second that passed increased the volume of intensity around me.

Tobey was smiling but had no inclination to talk. He would laugh at small moments, but he was clearly experiencing sensory overload. It was evident he was having a great time but needed to get away from the intensity of the downtown. He remained seated on the golf cart and wrapped himself in a cozy blanket.

Sushi! At last, we grabbed the food and hopped onto the golf cart. Tobey was noticeably quiet on the drive back. The mystery dose of mushrooms hit him hard. He wasn't unresponsive but it was clear that he was feeling a lot. We drove into the garage and went upstairs.

We were in no way ready to eat.

Chop sticks? Good luck.

Packets of soy sauce? Maybe next year.

Tobey didn't say a word and beelined straight to the couch and stared at the ceiling. After a short while, he rolled over and stared at the ground. Panic was showing on his face.

I whispered to Sara,

"I definitely gave him a lot. I mean, he did say he wanted to see some shit."

We silently laughed.

I was sitting at the table trying my hardest to eat with Sara. Each piece I picked up somehow or another ended up falling back onto the plate. My perceived motor functions mocked me as I tried my hardest to get the sushi into my mouth.

3 minutes passed.

5 minutes passed.

Out of nowhere—in my peripheral vision—Tobey jumped up off the couch and said loudly,

"Let's get goin!"

Without a chance for Sara and me to follow, he walked past the table and started walking downstairs, through the garage, and outside.

"Bro where are you going?!"

I asked, laughing and confused.

We followed and met him outside.

"Dude."

He said, in a laughing panic as he paced in a circle.

"I'm in the fight for my LIFE right now!"

Strangely, he had a smile on his face so the whole thing seemed funny. However, he was completely serious. He did his best to explain,

"I was laying on the couch, and I felt like I was fighting through something... but I don't know what. I knew if I stayed there, I would have like fell into the couch and died. So, I said hell no, I'm fighting this, and I went outside..."

"…I'm still fighting it! I'm going through something *right now*."

In a strange way, I understood. I understood the grip of crisis and not being able to escape. But I still laughed at him.

I sat down on the driveway floor and Sara sat with me. Tobey grabbed a skateboard and stayed close but skateboarded slowly in a circle around the group.

The whole ordeal was hilarious. Tobey described this "fight for his life" as Sara and I watched. We weren't laughing *at* him per se, we were laughing at the relatability of the scenario.

Since I took a variety of doses throughout the day, the effects came in waves of varying intensity. As I sat with Sara, I felt a growing intensity beginning to rise in my stomach. Out of nowhere, colors became incredibly prominent. My senses became overwhelmed with joy and laughter as I watched Tobey skate around in a panic. I suddenly began to laugh, hard. Slowly but surely this laugh overcame me into hysteria. I laughed harder than I had all day. And finally, a massive wave of laugher took over and sent me belting incredibly loud.

I was having a laugh attack. Then finally, a laughing crisis.

I laughed so hard that I frantically got up and squeezed out

the words,

"I have to go upstairs."

I ran toward the house and stumbled through the doorframe. I could barely see where I was going because my eyes were squinting from laughing so hard.

As soon as I entered the house, the belt of laughter came out like a scream,

" AHaHaHa!"

The laugh was so foreign that it caught even me by surprise. I carried out the hardest laugh of my life on the stairway to the point of crying. After a few moments, I collected myself with a few deep breaths and went back outside to sit next to Sara.

"Did you seriously just run inside to laugh in shame?!"

Indeed, I did.

Just then, Tobey stopped skateboarding and sat down next to us. He sprawled out like a starfish on the ground exclaimed,

"uuuugugghhhhh…

whhooooooo"

"Bro I just went through the battle of my LIFE and made it out!"

He sprawled out on the ground and looked at the sky in relief,

"You guys don't even KNOW what I just went through! I can't even explain it. I was just dealing something, and I was fighting! I made it out!"

It was relatable; we had been there before.

We sat, laid, and sprawled out on my driveway talking about our days-long experience. We were still on our trip but without a doubt the *hard* part was over. What exactly was Tobey going through? That's only for him to know.

We were tired after our adventure; luckily, we had food to eat. We finally went upstairs and ate our sushi.

It was delicious.

The Door, The Palace, & The Gods

- Mindset: The days leading up to this experience, I knew I had no emotional or mental baggage. I had no internal struggles or problems. I was content and ready for a journey consisting of about anything and everything. My mind felt safe.

- Setting: Cleveland National Forest, California. We took my camper van to an unplanned camp site in a heavily wooded area. The campsite had a fire pit in the center of a small circular clearing which gave us unimpeded view of the vast night sky.

- Dosage: 2.5 grams each.

- Date/Time: Summer. 8:22pm.

- Method of Ingestion: Ginger Tea poured on crushed mushrooms.

- Strain: Golden Teachers.

Event -

This was a very loosely planned trip—we didn't know exactly where we were headed, but we had everything we needed for an experience. I've always desired a night journey. I wanted to stargaze under the vast night sky and watch the cosmos to unveil itself. When, where, and how? I didn't know yet.

I invited two friends and a babysitter in the days leading up to the event. Naturally, our plan changed as we got closer to the weekend. Originally, we planned to go to Las Vegas but that was quickly taken off the table after realizing that *shrooms* and crowds don't mix. Then, we planned on going to Anza-Borrego Desert, but the temperature was too hot. Finally, we concluded on Cleveland National Forest. It met the mark on what we were looking for as far as setting.

We packed the van with everything we needed: blankets, air mattresses, tents, food, and of course mushrooms. We arrived at the Observatory Campground at 7:30 p.m. and found a secluded spot where we wouldn't be bothered. Somehow with our impromptu planning, we made it to our destination. Our babysitter, Sara, gathered firewood with Eric while Tobey and I set up the area. We laid out a large bedsheet and chairs surrounding the fire pit. I started the fire and Eric got the music set up.

Earlier in the day I lost a bet with Tobey. The outcome of the bet was I had to wear a XXXL gray t-shirt/dress throughout the entire day and night. As far as bets go, this wasn't too bad—at least I was comfortable. The t-shirt stretched down below my knees while the sleeves surpassed my elbows; it had large metallic rainbow letters in the center that said "MAKE TODAY AMAZING". I looked ridiculous.

-

I brewed the tea, and I could feel the slight nervousness of the group. 2.5 grams is quite the dose, especially at night after a day of work. This was Eric and Tobey's second real mushroom experience; naturally, their nerves were showing. We all had our cups of mushroom and ginger brew and we cheers'd. Before we took our gulps, I gave a tiny pep talk to clear the nerves.

"Remember, you're going to feel weird, but that's the point, right? If you feel funky, don't fight it and see where it takes you. Don't panic—it'll all be over in a few hours. I love you guys."

I usually end my pre-trip cheers with a cheesy "I love you." It tends to lighten the mood. We drank our cups and settled in around the fire. Eric put on an *easy-going* playlist with classics and calming acoustics.

There's no going back now.

To me, the hardest part is actually ingesting the mushrooms. Strangely, I find comfort in *no going back.* I equate it to getting on a roller coaster. While sitting in the seat, you're terrified—but the ride itself is a blast. Any moment leading up to any event is typically the scariest part.

The fire gave us light, which illuminated our surroundings. The fire lit a variety of large trees circling us. At 9:00 p.m. on the dot, we saw our first signs of life.

"Yeah, I'm starting to feel it."

I can't recall if Eric or Tobey said it.

Eric and Tobey moved to the bedsheet on the floor to brace themselves for the come-up. I looked around the surrounding area and *felt* things differently. *Everything* around me started to get hazy. Not blurry, not strange, not scary, just different. I too needed to brace myself. I stood up and laid with them and looked at the night sky. My jaw, gone. Figuratively gone...

Right?

My ability to talk fell to near zero. I could speak but it was almost completely undesirable. The night sky above warmed me with impossible beauty. The large tree to my left. Intense.

Massively intense.

Tree, big.

It became too much. The tree was too intense. The build up was beginning to rise quickly. I felt nerves and intensity firing through my insides. Nervousness and paranoia reached the tipping point of explosion.

Woah.

Hold on.

Stop please.

Slow down.

Tree.

Tree.

Oh no.

This is too much.

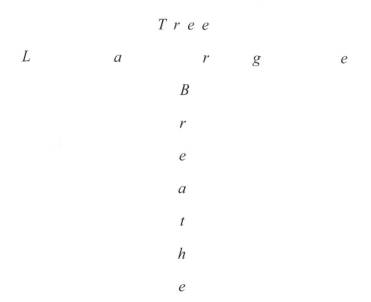

T r e e

L   *a*   *r*   *g*   *e*

B

r

e

a

t

h

e

Relax.

I closed my eyes and took a deep breath.

This feeling was the gift. This is what I wanted. I could feel the energy of every living thing around me—which was everything. I could feel the intensity of the nerves around me. I could feel Tobey and Eric incredibly overwhelmed, and I felt the magnitude of the earth and it was very close to being *too* much... So, I repeated my thoughts out loud for them and for *me*.

"How lucky are we....

We get to experience this for 4 more hours. We get to experience this gift. Look at the beauty around us. We can't fight it. We have to accept it. We have to breathe, relax, and accept it."

I took another deep breath.

It worked, thank god!

I was able to push through. Things were intense, but now I was comfortable with it. A wash of relief poured over my entire body. I was both sober and not. My muscles relaxed and all nervousness and paranoia left immediately. I knew that I was okay. I felt okay with the distortions and embraced them. The new world unveiled itself and more importantly, so did the cosmos.

I was now ready for the tree on my left. I looked at the base and followed it up to the brightly illuminated branches which led to the leaves. The leaves, however, were pronounced. They were massive. They were snowflakes? Or at least what I could correlate to the shape of snowflakes. They were physical forms of geometric shards, pointing with the false identity of leaves. Each leaf and branch became fractal shards part of a whole. They were structured, rigid, and they were beautiful.

The tree to my right, pine needles caught my eye.

Pine needles?

Thousands of them. Too many to count. Again, with the false identity of pine needles. I watched them slowly become blurred. They blended into fuzzy oil-painting frays. They, along with the snowflake tree to my left, were impossibly themselves so much so, that they no longer were what I knew them to be. They merely existed in the eternal all-ness of the forest and the earth. They, simply, were *it*-selves with only neutral it-ness.

They, were, trees.

I turned to Eric and pointed at the fanned blurry pine needles and described what I was seeing. He followed my direction up the tree. I described the fuzz which he also strangely saw. Did I manifest his vision to see what I was describing? Or did he see what I saw through his eyes? Impossible to tell.

I looked past the illuminated trees to the night sky. The sky graciously showed itself back to me. The sky was no longer an endless shapeless horizon. It had structure. It took form into a vast tufted dome and what I can only describe as grid-squares. The tufted points pulled space back into, well, more space. Endless massive tufted pulled stars into the backdrop of oblivion. Beauty. Stars were brighter and clearer, and the night sky morphed into a closer version of itself.

I thought,

"Can I pull it down?"

I pictured myself pulling the sky down toward me with a rope and the sky obliged. The sky pulled in toward me and stopped where the treetops met the sky. The dome was close. Space was now within reach.

Impossibly close.

Can I climb a ladder and touch the ceiling of what we call the night sky?

Absolutely.

Do I have the will power?

No.

I had to pee. I stood up and realized my ridiculous outfit. The large t-shirt dress now became part of me. I don't know if the t-shirt personified me, or if I added to it, but my body moved in it like a lost elderly woman in the woods. My arms were flimsy, my hands were weightless and swayed with my movements, and my feet were bare. I grabbed my lantern and frolicked to the edge of camp where the shrubs met the dirt.

A hundred.

No, a thousand.

No, countless shrubs of dandelion type floral weeds

stretched from my feet to the deep forest. The darkness had completely surrounded me; yet I was comfortable. I squatted to get eye level with the endless rows of seemingly strategically placed shrubs. They swayed and breathed in every direction in the nonexistent wind. I stayed and appreciated them in silence.

I turned back and saw the group around the fire as I wandered through the shrubs. At that moment, they were the only visible light in the entire universe. They were floating in deep space around the fire and didn't even know it. They were alive and I felt them. I walked back and sat down near Eric.

We all talked, laughed, and described our visuals. Tobey, however, fell silent.

"How you doin' man?"

I asked as I sat next to him.

Silence.

Then, finally a response,

"Dude this is roughhhh….

I'm having a tough time."

Silence.

He continued.

"I'm a burden. I rely on the people around me for comfort. I can't be alone......

I'm having a rough time man."

Silence.

"Dude this is rough. I feel like I'm going through something and it's hard. I feel like I can't make it stop. I feel like I can't get passed this. I need to feel you next to me.

Can you sit next to me and rub my back?"

Tobey was clearly having a tough time. His face, stale and sad. He was indeed, going through a crisis. I sat down and he immediately scooted next to me. He needed physical contact. He needed to feel. I touched his back and he exhaled with relief; however, his crisis continued, and he fell silent.

I had empathy. I felt for him; we all did, but unfortunately for Tobey, I could not relate to his struggle and neither could Eric. We ...were just having...way too much fun! Everything around us was profound. Everything was brilliant—everything was wonderful! We were getting lost in the fire and beauty of the natural world around us. Our attempts to pull him out fell short, so it became clear to us that he had to just deal with it.

The fire started dwindling, so Sara brought all of our available light sources around the fire. We had flashlights, battery powered lanterns, clip on book lights, and most importantly we had a tiny 3" x 5" dollar store portable light rectangle. The light sources were strategically placed around Tobey to provide additional comfort.

Tobey hadn't moved or talked for a while. He was leaning back on a cushion and staring at the tiny light rectangle. We watched him and wondered what was going on in his brain.

He snapped out of his trance and spoke,

"Can you put on more of a techno type song?"

I was excited and exclaimed,

"Bro you're alive!!!"

Eric put on a techno type song and Tobey fell back into his trance. He stared. He stared at the light rectangle for the entirety of the song and spoke again with a massive smile,

"Bro you guys don't even know about that light!"

He said, referencing the light rectangle,

"It's a door. The light turned into a door. I just cried that whole time. It was so beautiful."

He was back and no longer in crisis mode. He was enjoying his door. I asked,

"What do you see? Like, describe it to us."

He replied,

"Leave me and..meoodoo.."

He stuttered,

He wanted to say, "Leave me and my door alone" but that's not what came out.

"Leave me and meodoor alone! I mean, my door not, meo-door. Fuck it, it's Meo Door. Leave me and Meo Door alone!"

It was now Meo Door and it belonged to Tobey. He listened to music and stared at Meo Door, song after song. He swore that it was the craziest thing he'd ever seen. He described it as a vast desert scene with a large illuminated Meo Door at the center. After enjoying it for a while, he convinced me to take his place. Tobey stood for the first time in what felt like years and set up my body position to see what he saw.

I took his spot and got comfortable. I stared and listened to the pulsating techno shaking the light rectangle. Slowly but surely, I saw it. It became a door— Meo Door. It breathed and changed size.

It became large and I became small. The vibrant futuristic light turned into something from a different timeline… or space? I continued to look and before I knew it, I closed my eyes. With my eyes closed, I saw the outline of the door. I don't know if I went through the door or if the door even had anything to do with it, but I was now in a room, in a foreign place.

I was in a large dark black room with illuminated red faces. The room went on forever with endless space warping slowing in any and every direction. There was no floor, ceilings, or walls. There was just space and morphed pillars of boundless color and shapes. Faces made up everything in sight. Faces with no beginning or end, warping and undulating clockwise. The faces were eternal and still. Encompassing life in red-lined beauty, these were the gods, and they knew I was there. I said it out loud,

"I've seen the room of the gods."

I opened my eyes and the whole group was looking at me.

"Okay yeah, Tobey's right, that shit is crazy."

I stood up again to wander. I walked back into the darkness overlooking the rows of breathing weeds. I turned around and saw the group surrounding the fire and the van in the background. The van looked cozier and cozier the longer I looked. I felt myself becoming more and more tired as I stared at my bed inside the van. I walked past the group and climbed into the van. I laid on top of the bed and stared at the breathing ceiling. I closed my eyes and was immediately in a different place.

The entity that is *me* floated down a beautiful vast mountain side. *I* stopped floating down near the tree line which led me facing a massive spinning place. The palace was surrounded by large pillars with bulbous spinning domes in a Mughal building fashion. The ornament bulbs were spinning at similar speeds in every and all morphed directions. An impossible amount of colorful spinning bulb pillars zoomed in toward me as I was engulfed inside the palace. The Palace no longer had description or dimensions. Inside I felt red swirling eyes moving slowing in omnidirectional paths to nowhere. I was in a state of calm bliss enjoying the visions.

Somewhere during the journeys into my psyche, I fell asleep. I was aware of being asleep while my consciousness was awake. The visual distortions were gone but the feelings of *being* were prevalent. I became aware that I was no longer here.

The next morning, I woke up to the beautiful views of the campground. Even more refreshing, I was conscious and sober. I now understood the absoluteness of my sober reality. To be sober and conscious in normalcy on earth is a gift which cannot be under-appreciated. Only those who have gone through the inability of self awareness while wandering through an uncontrollable reality can truly appreciate a stable sober mind.

The View

- Mindset: This was my friend Katie's first time using any sort of conscious altering drug. Naturally, I felt a sense of responsibility, so I had to be mentally prepared to take care of her. I believe the extra responsibility had a positive effect on my relaxed demeanor since I knew a self-crisis was out of the question. Mostly, I was excited to share this experience with three close friends.

- Setting: Our setting was a park in San Diego, California which looked over both the ocean and rolling hills. It had enough space where strangers would have to go out of their way to interact with our group. Our section of the park provided us a sense of comfortability along with the convenience of bathrooms and water fountains.

- Dosage: 1.5 grams each.

- Date/Time: Spring. 12:00pm.

- Method of Ingestion: Lemon TEK.

- Strain: Golden Teachers.

Event -

My good friends Sara, Caleb, and Katie came into town. Caleb had some experiences with psychedelics, but Katie not so much. This was her first time taking any true conscious altering drug. I gave her the standard *spiel* about how mushrooms are not that big of a deal. I explained how dosages work, and that we would most likely laugh, feel funky, and have a wonderful day outside. Whenever someone asks how long a mushrooms experience lasts, I typically say 4 hours. 4 hours is my go-to time frame because it's the longest I've ever felt anything. She had some questions but overall had little hesitation.

We settled on 1.5 grams. 1.5 grams is what I typically recommend for an introduction to mushrooms 101. The plan was similar to experiences I have had in the past—drink the mushrooms, go to a park, lay out with some blankets, and have a cooler full of snacks and goodies.

Fresh lemons. For whatever reason, whenever agreeing to take any sort of drug with a group of friends there is always a ceremonial aspect to it. *Fresh* lemons and a "cheers" are a necessary part of a mushroom tea ceremony. We drove to a nearby supermarket for the essential items like fresh fruit, water, snacks etc. When it came to the lemons, I precisely chose the ones that felt right. Under what qualifications? I do not know.

Back at my house, we packed our stuff and got the mushrooms soaking in the lemon juice. About 20 minutes later, I made ginger tea and poured it on top of the soaking mushrooms. We had to be quick after drinking our brew because the park was a 5-minute drive and we wanted to be sure there was no possibility that I would be driving under the influence.

Down the hatch.

We arrived at the park without any hiccups. The park was fairly large, and no one was wandering about. We searched for a spot that would be inconvenient for a stranger to stumble upon. We settled on a patch of grass half under a large tree, half in the sun, with an overlook to beautiful S. A trail sidewalk only 10 feet away serpentined around the whole park which led to bathrooms, the parking lot, and a children's playground. It was home base for the day. It was safe.

We brought every fuzzy blanket I owned to the park. We connected all of them with a slight overlap covering the grass and sat criss-cross. Katie and Sara started to crack jokes one after another as an undeniable mental defense mechanism. No matter how prepared you think you are to take a trip, walls are always put up during the come-up. Not by any grand measure, but still some sort of mental hesitation presents itself to slow the come-up.

She's beginning to feel it.

Katie said with a panicked smile and squinted eyes,

"I feel like I'm wet, but I can't tell if I am or not."

She looked at her hands and arms with a slight humorous confusion.

In sober life that statement would never be said. If you are wet, you know it without a doubt.

I told her,

"Oh yeah, you're starting to feel it!"

"No, no, no."

She shook her head and insisted she didn't feel anything at all. I was starting to feel it too.

Breathe.

The world in front of me began to lift. I held the curtain of my reality and stepped into tan world.

Tan. Heat. Earth.

I remember this place.

I took another deep breath to brace myself for the impact of my new reality. I hugged my own arms at the elbows and left them there for self comfort. I looked out far to my left and to my right as the group's noise began to fade away. The intensity of the come-up prevailed.

It's time to wander.

"I'm going on a walk, anyone coming?"

I asked.

I looked at the group, the two girls were shoeless, in their bathing suits, and in their own world. They looked at me like I was insane for even thinking about leaving the safe zone. They were comfortable and could not be convinced. Caleb on the other hand, looked like he was on the brink of crisis. He seemed relieved that I asked.

"Sure, I'll come!"

He said, trying to act casual.

We started to walk down the serpentine sidewalk. I asked him how he was feeling. As I asked, he looked incredibly relieved that I even asked the question. Regardless of how he was feeling before, he was relieved to get *anything* off his chest.

"Oh man I feel way better now."

He looked at me with a smiled relief.

It was a long pathway that zig-zagged around the park. We walked slowly, not in silence on purpose, but silence because it felt right. We could see Big Bear Mountain in the vast distance, or what we thought was Big Bear.

Snow caps.

White snowy tips which gradually faded into forest of lush greenery. The beauty stunned our senses and we stopped dead in our tracks at the same time. We felt confused at the shocking view, we turned to each other and asked,

"Has this view been here the whole time?"

It obviously had been but how did we not see it.

Why can we only appreciate the view on drugs?

As we were standing humbly in the presence of a god-like view, a noise came from behind us. Words were spoken. In horror, we turned around slowly and saw a stranger sitting on the bench looking at us.

Did he say something?

The stranger repeated himself,

"Beautiful isn't it?"

Sir, would you kindly mind your own fucking business.

Of course, I didn't say it, I would never. We looked

at him and then each other with the same confused look.

Do we have to answer?

We didn't even have to ask each other but we were both wondering the same thing.

Did that guy really say something or is it the mushrooms?

Caleb finally responded politely,

"Wait, what was that?"

The strange man started talking,

"Yep, I've been here for about 10 years. You can't really get much of a better view than that. You know, those mountains over there..."

He wouldn't stop. He kept talking and as he did, I tuned him out because I was in no condition to listen nor had the ability to articulate an appropriate answer.

He continued,

"It's so beautiful, especially this time of year when there are no clouds. Those mountains are typically not snowy this time of year. Do you know what's over there? It's Big Bear, ya ever been to Big Bear? _____"

We slowly walked away.

Caleb said with a humorous paranoia,

"What the fuck was that guy's problem. Can't he tell we're on mushrooms?"

We were back on the trail. It circled around and led to where the girls were, so we peaked over a small bend and saw them laughing.

Perfect, they don't need us.

Without saying anything we looked at each other and decided to keep exploring. Quietly and slowly, we wandered aimlessly looking at trees, shrubs, and flowers. Every so often one of us would take a deep breathe to soak in the experience. The serpentine walkway led us to a clearing at the end of the park which had an immense viewpoint. We got closer, and before we knew it, we froze in our tracks. Silently we stared until one of us was able to say something.

"Dude... do you see that?

…

What the hell."

Caleb said.

He was right, it was beautiful. It was also a lot to take in without the expectation of immense beauty. Why couldn't we always see like this? Why weren't we able to appreciate nature with a sober mind. Something, nothing, and everything about *this* reality was different. It had a different texture, color, intensity, existence. You could *feel* the overwhelmingness of the view.

How do I feel this view?

Cars in the distance drove up hills, buses were on their routes, people were walking on side walks... Trees, shrubs, terrain, clouds, sky—it was all there, and it was all existing with itself and only itself. I was only witnessing it exist. Each distant hill was on top of the next with and without the construct of space. I could not comprehend how you could see one hill behind the other. There is nothing normal about normalcy of dimensions. The logic of perception and perspective doesn't make sense there. Space, size, distance solely and simply *does not*, there.

The hill is bending.

It had to be in order for me to see another hill behind it.

Caleb and I stood in silence while gazing at the view. Finally, we turned to each other,

"Wow."

"Let's get the girls over here to see this."

We started walking back to our safe spot. The trail weaved in and out through the park paralleling some trees right off the trail.

I loosely grabbed my elbows to comfort myself as I wandered down the trail.

The trees became huge. Their intensity became beautiful which pulled me in to get a closer look. I walked up to a large tree and stood at its base looking up the trunk to admire the branches spouting from the body. It became clear to me that the branches were growing in the direction of the sun. Each branch trying to outgrow the other for a little extra sunlight. I knew this fact all my life but never really thought about it. Of course they were growing toward the sun, this was common knowledge. For some reason, witnessing their thirst for sun struck me. I felt their desire for light. I felt their need to grow at the sun. I started to notice that everything around me was growing at the sun. Including us, our buildings, homes, businesses, we're all trying to get closer to what gives us life. I contemplated this revelation as we arrived at home base.

"You guys HAVE to come see this view."

Classic. Classic person on drugs trying to share their experience with everyone. They both looked incredibly unamused, unphased, and uninterested in leaving the comforts of the blankets. After some serious debating, they were finally convinced. Without a care for our *stuff*, we walked down the path to the viewpoint. After 15 feet of walking, Sara and Katie were already commenting how nice it felt to walk around. So much to look at, so much beauty, so much *everything.*

Katie would periodically nervously comment on how she didn't *really* feel anything. She wasn't even convincing herself.

We talked until we reached the viewpoint. The conversations stopped abruptly as everyone noticed the overlook. Layers of hills and roads which made no sense to anyone stacked on and over each other. Our perceptions could not comprehend the distance from mountain to hill. Cars, lights, hills, ocean, beauty; it was almost too much beauty to handle. Caleb and I looked at each other, proud to be the ones responsible for sharing the beauty.

"See?"

Yes, they saw.

Seemingly alien, the view took my breath away once again. The roads leading to other roads were impossible to comprehend. The busyness of normal life was incredibly entertaining to witness. The hills led to an ocean backdrop, which had an infinite view of vast colored sea water. The view was unobtainable. It was impossible to measure in terms of vastness and complexity. Yet, we witnessed it and had the ability to enjoy it the way it was meant to be appreciated. Colors were colors in the most intricate and delicate possibility. Ombre, hue, and light, capitulated any possible comprehension of what is and what is not. The view, again, was itself and only existed. The view, was.

We wandered back to the trail and stopped by the bathrooms. The restrooms were built with cinder blocks and cheap paint which made the building feel lifeless. However, Katie and Sara gave it life. Caleb and I watched the girls struggle to figure out how to use the restroom door and navigate the stalls. Luckily for us, the restroom had shoulder high see-through cinderblock holes which allowed Caleb and I to laugh at confusion which ensued within the women's bathroom.

We wandered back on the trail and eventually made it back to our home base. Slowly but surely, the world's reality drifted back into normalcy. The confusion of beauty and intensity became achievable. Distances of hills and mountains became fathomable and the structure of space became possible. The mushrooms had come and left but what remained was an appreciation for the life around us.

It was lovely.

The Toe

- Mindset: Calm. Meditative. Spiritual.

- Setting: Home, San Diego, California.

- Dosage: 0.5 grams (each). This is an example of why it's important to never underestimate the power of the mushroom.

- Date/Time: Fall. 6:40 p.m.

- Method of Ingestion: Ginger tea.

- Strain: Golden Teachers.

Event -

This trip wasn't planned. And, if you would have asked me before this experience what a person would feel after ingesting 0.5 grams of psychedelic mushrooms, I would say almost nothing. That's because 0.5 grams is a microdose—right?

Sara and I hadn't *done* mushrooms in quite a while—together at least—I had done quite a lot on my own (obviously). We were watching TV at my house after a long day of errands when Sara asked,

"What if we took a microdose and did yoga?"

I was pleasantly surprised because the last time Sara had *done* mushrooms was when we each took 4.2 grams [The Spiral]. After that incredibly painful event, I thought her days of exploring her psyche were over. To her, this was a good way to dip her *toe* back in.

To me, deciding to *do* mushrooms is much simpler. I agreed to take them because, well, it was a Saturday.

Sara put on the tea kettle and I weighed precisely 0.5 grams of mushrooms, which looked incredibly small. 0.5 grams looks as if you held two weightless pennies in the palm of your hand. 0.5 grams is in fact so small, that I had to snap off the mushroom stems because they weighed too much. What was left? Two, tiny, spectacularly small, mushroom caps.

After grinding the *shrooms* into a fine powder, we mixed them into our teas and drank them quickly. Surprisingly, the fine powder mixed in nicely with our teas and was quite delicious. After a soothing 20-minute yoga session, our attention moved to getting food ready for dinner.

Halfway through cooking the come-up took us both by surprise. A halting panic sunk into my stomach and slight paranoia set in.

But I only took half a gram?

My living room bathroom has black artistic "X's" painted on the wall. Each X stretches from wall to wall in rows and columns. I went to use the bathroom and as I stood there, I noticed a subtle glowing blue neon strip pulsing over the row of X's. I was a little shocked to have visuals after such a light dose!

"I'm seeing shit different! I'm totally having visuals!"

I yelled to Sara from the bathroom.

"Okay, I didn't want to say anything, but ME TOO!"

Somehow or another, the small amount of mushrooms we digested happened to be impressively potent. I never thought a half of a gram could be so powerful but here we were, tripping hard.

I exited the bathroom and looked at Sara. Her face was flushed red and her nose was runny. Having gone on mushroom journeys with her in the past, I knew this only happens when she takes large doses.

We started to cook food, but it became increasingly difficult to accomplish. Somehow, I found myself mixing some sort of polenta on the stove. Abrupt hysterical laughter followed and every move either of us made became grossly hilarious—clear signs of an intense mushroom journey to come.

The onset of laziness hit me with the fury of a thousand slugs and my body became very difficult to move. I took my plate to the couch and sat down. I lifted my plate to see *exactly* what I was going to put into my body. After holding my plate at eye-level, I decided that it was far too intense to look at while eating. I then forgot how to accurately put food on my spoon. I gripped the handle like a toddler and opened my mouth incredibly wide just to make sure I didn't miss.

"Well, I guess were having a full journey. What should we do?"

Sara said.

"Let's go explore!"

We hopped off the couch and went downstairs toward the garage. I opened the door and there was nothing but pure darkness. Hesitantly (scared), we slowly poked our heads into the darkness. Our eyes widened as we couldn't see anything and I quickly turned on the lights. Luckily, the garage still existed, and a wash of relief came rushing over us.

We laughed.

We slowly walked onto the cold concrete floor as if it was a strange and ominous area. We turned the corner, and two spiders were hanging near each other in front of the windowsill.

In silence, we watched them.

One of the spiders was thick, dark, and seemingly *bad*. The other was skinny, lanky, and seemingly *good*. The bad spider crept its way closer to the good one. In fear for the good one, we quietly gasped and waited for the attack, but he was *ready*. They punched each other dramatically trying to gain the advantageous position. Flickering their impossibly tiny limbs at each other, they battled. Triumph! The good spider defended his web unscathed!

We were ecstatic.

   "What if we opened the garage and explored outside?"

I said and she agreed.

We opened the garage door and again, we hesitantly poked our heads into unfamiliar territory. We stepped onto the driveway and looked at the massive structures around us. Amidst our gaze, headlights shined from around the corner. Sara and I looked at each other in a frenzy and sprinted back into the garage and closed the door!

We had enough adventure.

We decided to get as comfortable as possible, so we changed into pajamas. Lazily, I sat on the floor trying my best to get into my profoundly soft fuzzy pajama bottoms. I had an itch on the bottom of my foot, so I grabbed my ankle and brought it forward.

My big toe is different.

I leaned forward and inspected the marvelous entity that was my toe. My skin, or rather at the time, *the* skin, was no such thing. The creases and crevasses on the bottom of my left toe were prolifically vast. Caverns and trails swirled into a honeycomb of holes and structures that went on for lifetimes. The deserted plains of a once seemingly vast flourishing environment were now empty rigid mountains and caverns of unfathomable density. These mountains existed on, in, and through, the bottom of my left toe. I was lost in it. Purely captivated and in awe in the seemingly once inhabited vast desert that was—Toe.

I couldn't believe it. So, I showed it to Sara,

"Look at the bottom of my toe."

Unphased, she did.

"What the hell is all that?!"

She witnessed it just as I did.

Shadows and creases were so incredibly vast that one had

to wonder where all this space came from? Moreover, where had this space been all my life. The entity that is *I* had to have been aware at some point that a massive mountain range of complex contour lines existed on a portion of *my* body. The answer was simple; this body is in no way the entity with consciousness. The same relationship which exists between a human being and his or her car, is the same in relationship *we* have with *ourselves*.

Even more unfortunate, we treat our bodies with much less importance than we do our cars.

We moved to the couch, and I laid back in bliss. I closed my eyes, curiously, to see what adventures existed internally. I watched and waited until I *felt* shadow-green bushes and foliage in the center of my closed eye. The foliage began to slowly ruffle, and a man's face emerged from the brush. The man was what I would describe to be seemingly American Indian. He was slowly moving moving left and right with the foliage.

He was beautiful in essence. There is no other description for this man as he doesn't exist in this place. I *felt* him rather than *seeing* him. His description can only be felt, never witnessed, as *he* does not exist on this plane.

I don't know his purpose, nor did I feel an underlying message, but I was grateful he was there. *Seeing* him was a gift of some sort that I have not yet been able to determine.

I opened my eyes and stood up to grab a drink of water.

There was a painting with every color imaginable behind the couch I was laying on. As I stood up, the painting grabbed my attention. After a few seconds of wondering what was different, I felt as if I was noticing new colors.

-

I have red-green colorblindness (deuteranomaly). This form of colorblindness makes green look redder due to damage to the brain or damage to cone cells in the eye…. (more or less—I'm not an eye doctor).

-

I was in shock and immediately my eyes began to water.

"Oh my god, what's wrong?"

Sara asked.

"It's the painting. I can see some of the colors now in a way I couldn't before."

I started to name greens, grays, blues, and reds, which had been blended before. I showed her that I could precisely identify the colors and exactly where they blended. I stood on the couch to get even closer and more tears filled my eyes. It was as if I could see colors that had previously been blended. It was a gift of proof—colors that I thought I would never see existed!

I was grateful.

Our microdose (barely) began to slowly fade away. For the rest of the evening, Sara and I laid on the couch and watched TV and talked about our spontaneous journey.

Eventually, we fell asleep.

*This story was written after I developed my graph explaining dosages. Time and time again, mushrooms have sent me back to edit and reevaluate what I think of dosages.

Key takeaway— never underestimate the mushroom.

The Observer

- Mindset: Nervous. I hadn't *done* mushrooms in quite a while. Since my last trip, I somehow fell victim to the same misinformation I've tried so hard to teach people to avoid. It's easy to be convinced by the propaganda and forget just how gentle psychedelic mushrooms can be. I felt so much anxiety before ingesting that I contemplated not even taking them. I'm glad that I did.

- Setting: Sara's family home, West Palm Beach, Florida.

- Dosage: 3.0 grams.

- Date/Time: The eve of a very popular winter holiday. Exactly one year after my first trip [The Cuddle Bug]. 3:42 p.m.

- Method of Ingestion: Crumbled mushrooms in ginger tea.

- Strain: Golden Teachers.

Event –

It had been almost one year since my first ever mushroom experience. I had the idea to celebrate the one-year anniversary with the people who made it happen—Sara, Hunter, Jon, and Emily. I asked Sara if she would be okay with hosting a celebratory mushroom experience at the very place where this adventure began. Her family graciously agreed.

Jon and Emily [The Cuddle Bug] were directly responsible for not only this book, but for my life. Before their gift of 1.5 grams of an unknown strain of psilocybin mushrooms, I was certainly lost, and I felt my death was coming. So, as a celebration of life, I pitched them the idea and the date was set in stone.

- -

Hunter and I woke up and almost immediately we started to prep Sara's home for the experience. We hopped in his truck and went to the closest Home Depot for firewood, chairs, and tiki torches to create a relaxed environment outside. Sara's family home is situated on 2 acres of property surrounded by lush greenery and forests. Just outside the perimeter, tall endless pine trees stretched on for miles.

From the moment I woke up, I felt a heavy weight of anxiety in the pit of my stomach. Even to this day, I still don't know why I felt so nervous.

Well, 3.0 grams is a lot.

Hunter and I set up chairs around the fire pit and surrounded the hearth with tiki torches. Even with a sober mind, the yard looked awesome.

Jon and Emily arrived and greeted Sara's family while I weighed the doses. Hunter and I decided to take 3.0 grams while Jon agreed on 2.0 grams and Emily decided on 1.65 grams.

Grinding mushrooms into a fine powder then mixing them into a tea often results in an intense come-up which I was too nervous to handle. Instead, I decided to crumble up the mushrooms into larger pieces and soak them in my tea. Sara sensed my pre-flight jitters and kept me at arms distance before the trip began.

Please be gentle.

At 3:42 p.m., we all drank our tea.

The sky had mixed emotions that day. It was sunny, then cloudy, then sprinkled, then windy, and then sunny again. Luckily, Hunter had everything we needed for the experience, including a pop-up pavilion we could move our chairs under in case it rained. Jon, Emily, and I got comfortable in our areas to prepare for the come-up. Emily laid out a cozy blanket on the grass and sage-smoked herself for a spiritual cleansing.

Jon sat in his chair and pretended not to look nervous.

Hunter, however, was acting just how we expected him to—calm, cool, and collected while doing yard work and playing with his German-Shepard, Clover. Impressively unphased after taking 3.0 grams.

I turned on music to set the mood straight by playing 70's classic psychedelic rock.

"I feel like we're doing exactly what our parents generation was doing at this age."

Emily said.

"You're so right! I feel like we belong in the 70's right now."

I replied.

The mood was certainly set, and the group was surrendering to the experience. We all sat and laid quietly in our own areas peacefully watching the sky and listening to music.

My nervousness began to fade as I sat and admired the massive clouds above. The idea of anxiety vanished and seemed almost silly. The come-up arrived and was much gentler than any other experience I've ever had. Blissful existence are the closest words I could ever try to express. My body reached a point of ultimate relaxation and presentness.

All it took was one deep breathe; I became the observer. A tourist in a place where every human being on earth longs to be. There was no possibility of stress or worry. The idea of anxiety became more foreign than any other self-induced irrational fear. It became clear that those problems are shortfalls of human existence and were not allowed in this perspective. I was merely a passenger in a vessel experiencing the skyline the same way the dead feel witnessing the unveiling of the heavens.

The heavens were there. The clouds rushed away and opened up a part of the atmosphere—a part only available to those who choose to live. Pure light shined on distant clouds so massive that their size is only comparable to the colossal.

Light, color, bliss.

"Wow guys, are you seeing this?"

I said.

"Oh yeah."

Jon said, whose chair was now facing the direction of distant clouds.

I looked straight up into the sky above.

Thick massive bold lines became evident. Kaleidoscope snowflakes, perfectly still, encompassed the geometric makeup of what we call clouds. My world was now truly psychedelic.

"How about the patterns in the clouds? Do you see them? They look like snowflakes, right?"

I asked Jon.

"Yeah, I think I know what you mean."

Jon said, clearly not knowing what I meant.

The lines stretched out to the horizon making up the entire sky. I was lost in them, marveling at the beauty, experiencing them as the objective grateful observer.

Hunter walked up and everything began to change. His presence snapped us all back into reality. He approached with a smile and threw cardboard into the fire.

Emily sat up from her blanket and was pulled back into normalcy. Jon too, turned around and looked at Hunter throwing boxes into the fire. My attention now moved to the busyness around the group.

Hunter quickly jumped on the ATV and turned it on which created a loud roar.

At the same time, Emily noticed that one of the cardboard boxes in the fire had a large lizard on it! She stood up quickly to save it. Jon noticed the commotion and saw the lizard about to go up in flames.

"Oh my god! There's a lizard in the fire!"

Jon said.

Emily quickly fished out the lizard by grabbing the charred box with the lizard standing proud.

Jon looked at me and said,

"Dude did you see the lizard?! Dude look!"

Hunter cranks his ATV at full velocity and jets across the yard letting off an even louder roar. Clover ran along side him and tried to bite the tires of his ATV. Hunter almost struck Clover with the ATV in a dramatic, intense scene. Amidst the commotion, Emily walked to over me with the box in her hand and with the lizard looking right at me. This became too much, and I experienced a sensory overload.

"Ahh!!"

I screamed, laughed, and dodged the lizard. At that very moment, "Hooked on a Feeling" by Blue Swede started playing on blast. If you know the tune, you know that the first 34 seconds of the song is a group of deep voices yelling,

"Ooga-Chaka Ooga Ooga"

Over and over and over again.

I looked at Jon and Emily after dodging the lizard and said,

"Jesus Christ this just got really intense!"

We all laughed!

I eagerly changed the music, and we all watched Hunter on the ATV zooming across the yard.

"How the hell is he doing all that right now?"

I said.

"That's legend status bro. He knows exactly what he's doing."

Emily said.

We all naturally went back to our cozy spots. Emily laid on the blanket while Jon and I sat down in our chairs. We were very easily sucked back into mushroom world.

I sat back in my chair and watched the large pine trees. The frays from the pine needles became fuzzy as they were during my Cleveland trip with Eric and Tobey. It brought me joy seeing a familiar landscape.

The wind started to blow at the level of treetops—or at least it seemed like they were. Hundreds of tall, skinny pine trees bended and swayed left and right in no organized fashion. The sky opened up and displayed a space large enough for a god. The pine trees danced seemingly happy while the gift of the sky pushed on forever.

My legs were no longer there.

I was no longer in my body.

Once again, I became the observer.

I felt a wash of gratitude fall over my soul. Fear was the first thing that entered my mind. Fear, in this state, is one of the most ludicrous sounding ideas ever cultivated by man. It felt impossible that fear could ever hold me back.

Fear of disappointment. Fear of mushrooms. Fear of death. Fear of pain. Fear, in its simplest form, was no longer part of my life. I was now resting, and my soul entered bliss. Never in my life have I rested more purely or without worry. I became *bliss*.

It started to rain.

Hunter walked back to the group from the other side of the house and pulled his chair under the pop-up pavilion. Jon, Emily, and I gathered our things and took cover with him.

I asked Hunter (who suffers from anxiety) if he too felt freedom.

"I don't feel any of that stuff. I don't feel stress. I don't feel anxiety, I don't hear any voices in my head. Nothing. Just rest."

I could relate to it more than he could possibly know. I've spent every day of my life in a constant forward motion. The first part of my day begins with a sudden desire to start moving. It's like a voice, or drive, in my mind telling be to do better and to accomplish something. If I sit down for too long or if I want to rest, I am stopped by my own conscious telling me to *get something done.* If I'm not in a constant motion, anxiousness fills my chest and the desire to jump out of my own skin grows into an unbearable itch. It's exhausting and mostly, it makes it difficult to sleep.

But that weight didn't exist anymore. I was able to forget *knowing* what anxiety is. Anxiousness, fear, death all became self-made obstacles that were incomprehensible to the observer. More than anything, I was at peace.

As it rained, the four of us remained huddled under a small pop-up tent.

I said to the group,

"Isn't it strange that there is a warm dry house ten feet away, but we would all rather be outside in the rain?"

The group smiled and it was clear they knew what I meant.

The music stopped and we all sat in silence listening to the rainfall. No one said a word, but we all shared a common appreciation for the nature around us.

The rain stopped and we once again moved around

the fire. The sun had set, and darkness took over our surroundings. Tiki torches and the fire pit became our main source of light. Somehow or another, the music was back on and a happy energy surrounded the group.

I began to reminisce through my memories of the past year and how they led me to the present. I looked up at the dancing silhouettes of pine trees swaying beautifully as if they were trying to get my attention. The fire's glow reflected on the droplets scattered through thousands of blades of grass throughout the yard—as glowing mist. Everything around me was hazy and beautiful.

"I'm going to wander."

I said to the group, as I stood up.

As I walked toward the darkness, I grabbed the last tiki torch and held it as a lifeline. I wandered to the edge of the property and could see the group around the fire. The path led me to silence outside the view of the group. I stood near a bundle of trees and squatted down to embrace my environment. As I sat in silence, I watched the tiny insects below me living in a world I could never truly understand.

The moon peaked out from the clouds and illuminated the entire yard. I finally felt what it was like to be in a forest with no sound because there was no one around to hear it. There is something desirable about existence without strings attached. It felt like absolute truth—no need for questions, no need for answers. I realized that the landscape around me lived without suffering—it simply, lived. I was able to comprehend this truth because I was no longer suffering, no longer burdening. My existence as a human being is in constant suffering. Pain by fear, by past, and by the unknown. This fear I had known my whole life, was me. All my suffering was my own doing.

This fear, luckily, can easily be replaced with love.

I stood up and walked back toward home base. It felt like the darkness spat me back out and I was once again in the land of the living, but this time with knowledge. Emily stood up and grabbed a torch to wander with Jon. The scene looked beautiful, so I snapped a photo to try and capture the essence. Jon and Emily went on their walk and Hunter went inside for the rest of the evening. After Jon and Emily returned, we sat by the fire and talked about our day. The general consensus was one of love and bliss—a spa day for the soul. Jon described his experience as simply "amazing".

The effects began to wear off and the three of us seemed to be fully energized and refreshed. As I walked inside for the night, Sara looked at me and said I was glowing.

I understood what she meant. I was loved, and I could love; all I had to do was try.

Happy 1 Year Anniversary.

This book was written over the course of a year. Since that time, I have experimented with high doses of psilocybin mushrooms and ingested a variety of different strains.

Each experience is truly special and vastly different than the rest — **love**, **death**, and **ego** being at the center of each one.

I don't know what my life would look like if I hadn't ingested that first gram of an unknown strain.

I'm just grateful that I did.

Glossary

Come-up - The nervous or rollercoaster type feeling when ingesting psilocybin containing mushrooms. This is often the first feeling or signs of effects.

Ego Death - Complete loss of subjective identity.

Fractals - A geometric figure where each part has the same statistical character as the whole. Examples include snowflakes, kaleido-scopes, or crystal growth.

Psilocybin - Chemical compound. 4-phosphoryloxy-N, N-dimethyl-ltryptamine. Psilocybin is the naturally occurring psychedelic prodrug compound in a variety of mushrooms species.

Psychoactive - Substances that when taken affect ones cognition or mental processes.

Psilocin - Chemical compound. The human body breaks down psilocybin and produces psilocin which causes psychedelic effects in the human body. Horses eat them too. Yes, horses trip.

Psilocybe Cubensis - Scientific name for the strain of psychedelic mushrooms.

TEK - Traditional Ecological Knowledge. Commonly referred to as TEK and often confused with technique.

Don't Panic - What you should do if you're panicking on mushrooms.

L. Alexander was born in 1991.

He currently resides in San Diego, California.

Cut these pages out

Reference them as needed

Dried Psilocybe Cubensis (in grams)

0.1 to 0.75 - Microdose.

You will feel capable to perform daily tasks.

You will likely feel a boost in creativity.

You will feel an enhanced appreciation for *things*.

You will likely feel agile, but odd, athletic ability.

You will know exactly what you are and are not capable of doing.

Regardless of the microdose, never underestimate the mushroom.

.75 to 1.5 - Introduction to Shroom world.

If you find yourself wanting to try psilocybin mushrooms but don't know how much to take...This is where you should start.

Things will seem different.

You feel it, but do you? You will ask yourself this throughout your ~ 4-hour experience. This will get you

comfortable with what if feels like on mushroom mountain.

You will feel your jaw but only a little.

Things that are beautiful will feel *more* beautiful.

You will likely feel comfortable and lazy.

You will have full but lackadaisical control of your body.

You will not want to talk to strangers.

You will laugh a lot.

You will see a lot.

You will feel a lot.

1.6 to 2.0 - This is where you should not start.

Things around you **will** be different.

You will feel different.

You may see patterns in everything, you may not. You will, however, see *something*.

Day to day will be enhanced and you will be 'wow'd'.

Your reality will not be the same reality as it was before you took mushrooms, but remember, this is what you wanted. You ate them, deal with it. You are on a trip and it will be beautiful.

2.1 to 3.5 - You've been on a trip but now you're going on a journey.

Your reality will be **very** distorted.

Fractals, geometric patterns, kaleidoscope, breathing, feeling colors - it's all here.

You will have control of your body, but you are clearly affected.

You will feel a lot.

You will find it difficult to speak.

Time, space, and reality will be very intense.

You will have a true psychedelic experience.

You will feel love.

You will feel intensity.

You will feel more than you thought you could feel.

I hope you have the courage.

3.6 to 4.1 - Major distortions in reality. Major distortions in self - possible ego death.

I wrote possible, but it's likely. You need to have a guide. You should have a guide for all of the above mentioned but for this one, you will **need** a guide.

Speech will be impeded, greatly.

You will have control of your body, but will you *really*?

You will question things around you because your reality is vastly different than anything you've ever known.

If you choose to close your eyes and lay back, don't panic, you are loved, and say goodbye to yourself.

Try and let go; you will be okay.

4.2 to 5.0 - Complete dissolving of self.

The patterns? Here.

Beautiful colors? Here.

But you won't really pay attention to them because you'll be too busy trying to deal with…everything.

Ego death.

Goodbye earth, you'll be back later.

Goodbye self, you'll be back later.

Have a qualified spiritual guide.

You will learn things about the universe that you cannot un-know.

5.1(+) - Likely paralysis. You ain't doin' much, bub.

You're gone, probably for a while.

No danger to your body, but make sure you leave it in a safe place because you will leave this place.